cooking with
chocolate

cooking with
chocolate

CHRISTINE FRANCE

HERMES
HOUSE

For all recipes, **quantites** are given in both **metric** and **imperial** measures and, where appropriate, measures are also given in **standard cups** and **spoons**. Follow one set but not a mixture because they are **not interchangeable**.

Standard **spoon** and **cup measures** are **level**.
1 tsp = 5ml, 1 tbsp = 15ml, 1 cup = 250ml/8 fl oz

Australian standard **tablespoons** are 20ml. Australian readers should use 3 tsp in place of 1 tbsp for measuring small quantites of gelatine, cornflour, salt etc.

Medium eggs are used unless otherwise stated.

The recipes in this book appeared previously as **Chocolate Ecstacy**.

First published in 1999 by Hermes House

© Anness Publishing Limited 1999

Hermes House is an imprint of Anness Publishing Limited
Hermes House, 88–89 Blackfriars Road, London SE1 8HA

ISBN 1-84038-501-4

A CIP catalogue record for this book is available from the British Library

Publisher Joanna Lorenz
Editor Sarah Ainley
Copy editors Linda Doeser and Jenni Fleetwood
Design Wherefore Art?
Photography Steve Baxter
Food for photography Jane Stevenson
Styling Diana Civil
Production controller Karina Han

Printed and bound in Singapore
1 3 5 7 9 10 8 6 4 2

cooking with chocolate

introduction

THE **IRRESISTIBLE** TASTE OF **DECADENCE**.

Few foods are as **rich**,
sensuous
and **wickedly tempting** as chocolate.
However you eat it – nibbled and savoured
or **downright indulgently** –
chocolate is **pure pleasure**.
For the cook, chocolate has a rare fascination.
It is a **sensitive** ingredient
which needs careful handling
but offers **remarkable rewards**.
The **velvety texture** and **rich flavour** adds
a touch of **luxury**
and there is something highly addictive
about this gift from the **gods,**
as anyone who has ever **tried to give it up**,
however briefly, will testify.

techniques

CHOCOLATE CAN BE **DIFFICULT** TO **HANDLE**, BUT THE WAY IT **LOOKS** AND **TASTES** IS **COMPENSATION** ENOUGH.

melting chocolate

USING A DOUBLE BOILER

Fill the base of a double boiler or saucepan quarter full with water. Fit the top pan or place a heatproof bowl over the saucepan. The water should not touch the top container. Bring the water to just below boiling point, then reduce to a slow simmer. Melt the chocolate in the top pan or bowl without stirring.

MELTING IN THE MICROWAVE

Break the chocolate into squares and place it in a microwave-proof bowl. Heat until just softened, checking often. Chocolate retains its shape when melted in this way.

DIRECT HEAT

Use only for recipes where the chocolate is melted in another liquid, such as milk or cream. Break up the chocolate into a saucepan and add the liquid. Heat gently, stirring occasionally, until the chocolate has melted and the mixture is smooth.

chocolate decorations

GRATED CHOCOLATE

Use a cheese grater to grate a large bar of chocolate. Grated chocolate is useful for sprinkling over desserts or coating the sides of gâteaux.

CHOCOLATE CURLS

Spread melted chocolate thinly over a cool work surface and leave to set. Push a metal scraper across the surface at an angle to remove long, thin chocolate shavings which should curl gently against the blade.

CARAQUE

Spread melted chocolate thinly over a cool work surface and leave to set. Using a cook's knife with a straight, rigid blade, pull the blade across the surface of the chocolate at an angle of 45 degrees to produce fine, curled shavings.

QUICK CURLS

Use a swivel-bladed vegetable peeler to shave short curls of chocolate from the whole bar. This method works best when the chocolate is at room temperature.

PIPED SHAPES

Spoon 15ml/1 tbsp melted chocolate into a piping bag, secure the top and snip the tip of the bag with scissors. Spread non-stick baking parchment on a cool work surface and pipe shapes. Leave the shapes to set before carefully lifting them off the paper. For curved shapes, place the paper over a rolling pin when setting the chocolate.

CHOCOLATE LEAVES

Paint the underside of a clean, dry and unblemished fresh leaf with an even coat of melted chocolate. Lay the leaf, chocolate-side up, on non-stick baking parchment and leave to set. When set, carefully peel away the fresh leaf to reveal the chocolate leaf.

FEATHERED OR MARBLED CHOCOLATE

Melt two contrasting colours of chocolate and spread one evenly over the cake or food surface to be decorated. Spoon the contrasting chocolate into a piping bag and pipe swirls over the chocolate. Working quickly before the chocolate sets, draw a cocktail stick through the swirls to create a feathered or marbled effect.

CUT-OUTS

Spread melted chocolate on a sheet of non-stick baking parchment and leave to set. Use a sharp knife to cut triangles or squares from the chocolate, or stamp out decorative shapes, such as hearts and flowers.

> ### cook's tip
> Chocolate keeps well if stored in a cool, dry place. Always check the "best before" dates on the pack.

Left from top, chocolate decorations: caraque, piped shapes, chocolate leaves, quick curls, chocolate curls.

chocolate ganache

A **LUXURIOUS**, CREAMY **FROSTING** FOR **GATEAUX** AND **DESSERTS**.

ingredients

enough to cover a 23cm/9in round cake

250ml/8fl oz/1 cup **double cream**

225g/8oz **plain chocolate**, broken into squares

method

1 Heat the cream and chocolate together in a saucepan over a low heat, stirring frequently until the chocolate has melted. Pour into a bowl, leave to cool, then whisk until the mixture begins to hold its shape.

chocolate fondant

THIS **ICING** GIVES A **SMOOTH FINISH** TO CELEBRATION **CAKES** AND CAN BE USED TO MAKE **SHAPES** AND **CUT-OUTS**.

ingredients

enough to cover a 23cm/9in round cake

350g/12oz **plain chocolate**, broken into squares

60ml/4 tbsp liquid **glucose**

2 **egg whites**

900g/2lb/7 cups **icing sugar**

method

1 Melt the chocolate with the glucose in a heatproof bowl over hot water.

2 Stir as the chocolate melts. Remove from the heat and allow to cool slightly.

3 In a clean, grease-free bowl, whisk the egg whites lightly, then stir into the chocolate mixture with about 45ml/3 tbsp of the icing sugar.

4 Using an electric mixer, gradually beat in enough of the remaining icing sugar to make a stiff paste. Wrap in clear film if not using immediately.

glossy chocolate sauce

DELICIOUS **POURED LIBERALLY** OVER **ICE CREAM**, OR ON **HOT** OR **COLD** DESSERTS.

ingredients

115g/4oz/1/2 cup **caster sugar**

60ml/4 tbsp **water**

175g/6oz **plain chocolate**, broken into squares

30ml/2 tbsp **unsalted butter**

30ml/2 tbsp **brandy** or **orange juice**

method

SERVES 6

1 Place the sugar and water in a saucepan and heat gently, stirring occasionally, until the sugar has dissolved.

2 Stir in the chocolate, a few squares at a time, until melted, then add the butter in the same way. Do not allow the sauce to boil. Stir in the brandy or orange juice and serve warm.

cook's tip

This sauce freezes well. Pour into a freezer-proof container, seal, label and freeze for up to 3 months.

white chocolate frosting

A FLUFFY, **RICH**, **WHITE** FROSTING TO ADD **SOPHISTICATION** TO **CAKES** AND **GATEAUX**.

ingredients

enough to cover a 20cm/8in round cake

175g/6oz **white chocolate**, broken into squares

75g/3oz/6 tbsp **unsalted butter**

115g/4oz/1 cup **icing sugar**

90ml/6 tbsp **double cream**

method

1 Melt the chocolate with the butter. Remove from the heat and beat in the icing sugar.

2 Whip the cream in a separate bowl until it holds its shape, then beat into the chocolate mixture. Allow to cool, stirring occasionally, until it begins to hold its shape. Use immediately.

cakes & bakes

cranberry & chocolate squares

MADE FOR **EACH OTHER** – THAT'S THE **CONTRASTING** FLAVOURS OF **TANGY-SHARP CRANBERRIES** AND **SWEET CHOCOLATE**.

ingredients

150g/5oz/1¼ cups **self-raising flour**, plus extra for dusting

115g/4oz/½ cup **unsalted butter**

60ml/4 tbsp **cocoa powder**

215g/7½oz/1¼ cups **light muscovado sugar**

2 **eggs**, beaten

115g/4oz/1⅓ cups fresh or thawed frozen **cranberries**

For the topping

150ml/¼ pint/⅔ cup **soured cream**

75g/3oz/6 tbsp **caster sugar**

30ml/2 tbsp **self-raising flour**

50g/2oz/4 tbsp soft **margarine**

1 **egg**, beaten

2.5ml/½ tsp **vanilla essence**

75ml/5 tbsp coarsely grated **plain chocolate**, for sprinkling

method

SERVES 12

1 Preheat the oven to 180°C/350°F/Gas 4. Grease an 18 x 27cm/7 x 10½in cake tin and dust lightly with flour. Combine the butter cocoa and sugar in a saucepan and stir over a low heat until melted and smooth.

2 Remove the melted mixture from the heat and stir in the flour and eggs, beating until thoroughly mixed. Stir in the cranberries, then spread the mixture in the prepared tin.

3 Make the topping by mixing all the ingredients in a bowl. Beat until smooth, then spread over the base.

4 Sprinkle with the grated chocolate and bake for 40–45 minutes, or until risen and firm. Cool in the tin, then cut into 12 squares.

chunky double chocolate cookies

KEEP THESE **LUSCIOUS TREATS** UNDER **LOCK** AND **KEY** UNLESS YOU'RE FEELING **GENEROUS**.

ingredients

115g/4oz/1½ cups **unsalted butter**, softened

115g/4oz/⅔ cup **light muscovado sugar**

1 **egg**

5ml/1 tsp **vanilla essence**

150g/5oz/1¼ cups **self-raising flour**

115g/4oz **plain chocolate**, roughly chopped

75g/3oz/¾ cup **porridge oats**

115g/4oz **white chocolate**, roughly chopped

method

SERVES 18–20

1 Preheat the oven to 190°C/375°F/Gas 5. Lightly grease two baking sheets. Cream the butter with the sugar in a bowl until pale and fluffy. Add the egg and vanilla essence and beat well.

2 Sift the flour over the mixture and fold in lightly with a metal spoon. Add the oats and chopped plain and white chocolate, and stir until evenly mixed.

3 Place small spoonfuls of the mixture in 18–20 rocky heaps on the baking sheets, leaving space for spreading.

4 Bake for 12–15 minutes or until the biscuits are beginning to turn pale golden. Cool for 2–3 minutes on the baking sheets, then lift on to wire racks to cool completely.

cook's tip
As a shortcut, substitute chocolate chips for the chopped chocolate. Chopped stem ginger would make a delicious addition as well.

double chocolate chip muffins

MARVELLOUS MUFFINS, PACKED WITH LOTS OF **CHUNKY** DARK AND WHITE **CHOCOLATE CHIPS**.

method

SERVES 16

1 Preheat the oven to 190°C/375°F/Gas 5. Place 16 paper muffin cases in muffin tins or deep patty tins. Sift the flour, baking powder and cocoa into a bowl and stir in the sugar. Make a well in the centre.

2 In a separate bowl, beat the eggs with the soured cream, milk and oil, then stir into the well in the dry ingredients. Mix together, gradually incorporating the flour mixture to make a thick and creamy batter.

3 Chop both the white and the plain chocolate into small pieces, then stir into the batter mixture.

4 Spoon the mixture into the muffin cases, filling them almost to the top. Bake for 25–30 minutes, until well risen and firm to the touch. Cool on a wire rack, then dust with cocoa powder.

---

cook's tip

If soured cream is not available, sour 150ml/¼ pint/⅔ cup single cream by stirring in 5ml/1 tsp lemon juice and letting the mixture stand until thickened.

---

ingredients

400g/14oz/3½ cups
plain flour
15ml/1 tbsp **baking powder**
30ml/2 tbsp **cocoa powder**
115g/4oz/¾ cup **dark muscovado sugar**
2 **eggs**
150ml/¼ pint/⅔ cup
soured cream
150ml/¼ pint/⅔ cup **milk**
60ml/4 tbsp **sunflower oil**
175g/6oz **white chocolate**
175g/6oz **plain chocolate**
cocoa powder, for dusting

MOIST, DARK AND **DEEPLY SATISFYING** – THIS HAS TO BE THE **ULTIMATE** CHOCOLATE **BROWNIE**.

ingredients

150g/5oz **plain chocolate**, broken into squares

120ml/4fl oz/½ cup **sunflower oil**

215g/7½oz/1¼ cups **light muscovado sugar**

2 **eggs**

5ml/1 tsp **vanilla essence**

65g/2½oz/⅔ cup **self-raising flour**

6ml/4 tbsp **cocoa powder**

75g/3oz/¾ cup chopped **walnuts** or **pecan nuts**

60ml/4tbsp **milk chocolate chips**

nut & chocolate chip brownies

method

MAKES 16

1 Preheat the oven to 180°C/350°F/Gas 4. Lightly grease a shallow 19cm/7½in square cake tin. Melt the plain chocolate in a heatproof bowl set over a pan of simmering water.

2 Beat the oil, sugar, eggs and vanilla essence together in a large bowl. Stir in the melted chocolate, then beat well until evenly mixed.

3 Sift the flour and cocoa powder into the chocolate mixture in the bowl and fold in thoroughly.

4 Stir in the chopped nuts and chocolate chips, tip into the prepared tin and spread evenly to the edges.

5 Bake for 30–35 minutes, or until the top is firm and crusty. Cool in the tin before cutting into squares.

cook's tip
These brownies will freeze for up to 3 months in an airtight container.

chocolate cinnamon doughnuts

SERVE THESE **LIGHT AND LUSCIOUS** TREATS **FRESHLY MADE** AND JUST **WARM**, SO THAT THE **CHOCOLATE** FILLING **MELTS IN YOUR MOUTH**.

ingredients

500g/1¼lb/5 cups **strong plain flour**
30ml/2 tbsp **cocoa powder**
2.5ml/½ tsp **salt**
1 sachet **easy-blend dried yeast**
300ml/½ pint/1¼ cups hand-hot **milk**
40g/1½oz/3 tbsp **butter**, melted
1 **egg**, beaten
115g/4oz **plain chocolate**, broken into 16 pieces
sunflower oil, for deep-frying

For the coating
45ml/3 tbsp **caster sugar**
15ml/1 tbsp **cocoa powder**
5ml/1 tsp **ground cinnamon**

cook's tip
Make sure the doughnuts are thoroughly drained on kitchen paper before rolling them in the coating, otherwise it will become sticky.

method

MAKES 16

1 Sift the flour, cocoa and salt together in a large bowl. Stir in the yeast. Make a well in the centre and add the milk, melted butter and egg. Stir, gradually incorporating the dry ingredients to make a soft and pliable dough.

2 Knead the dough on a lightly floured surface for about 5 minutes, until smooth and elastic. Return to the clean bowl, cover and leave in a warm place until the dough has doubled in bulk.

3 Knead the dough lightly again, then divide it into 16 pieces. Shape each into a round, press a piece of plain chocolate into the centre, then fold the dough over to enclose the filling, pressing firmly to make sure the edges are sealed. Re-shape the doughnuts when sealed, if necessary.

4 Heat the oil for deep-frying to 180°C/350°F or until a cube of dried bread browns in 30–45 seconds. Deep-fry the doughnuts in batches. As each doughnut rises and turns golden brown, turn it over carefully to cook the other side. Drain the cooked doughnuts well on kitchen paper.

5 To make the coating, mix the sugar, cocoa powder and cinnamon in a shallow bowl. Toss the doughnuts in the mixture to coat them evenly. Serve warm.

UNASHAMEDLY RICH AND **SWEET**, THESE BARS MAKE THE **PERFECT TREAT** FOR CHOCOHOLICS OF **ALL AGES**.

ingredients

225g/8oz/2 cups **plain flour**

2.5ml/½ tsp **baking powder**

115g/4oz/½ cup **unsalted butter**

50g/2oz/⅓ cup **light muscovado sugar**

150g/5oz **plain chocolate**, melted

30ml/2 tbsp **ground almonds**

For the topping

175g/6oz/¾ cup **unsalted butter**

115g/4oz/½ cup **caster sugar**

30ml/2 tbsp **golden syrup**

175ml/6fl oz/¾ cup **condensed milk**

150g/5oz/1¼ cups whole toasted **hazelnuts**

225g/8oz **plain chocolate**, broken into squares

chocolate butterscotch bars

method

MAKES 24

1 Preheat the oven to 160°C/325°F/Gas 3. Lightly grease a shallow 30 x 20cm/12 x 8in tin. Sift the flour and baking powder into a bowl.

2 Rub in the butter until the mixture resembles coarse breadcrumbs, then stir in the sugar. Work in the melted chocolate and ground almonds to make a light biscuit dough.

3 Press the dough evenly into the prepared tin, prick the surface with a fork and bake for 25–30 minutes until firm. Leave the cooked base to cool in the tin.

4 Make the topping. Mix the butter, sugar, golden syrup and condensed milk in a pan. Heat gently, stirring, until the butter and sugar have melted. Simmer, stirring occasionally, until golden, then stir in the toasted hazelnuts.

5 Pour the topping over the cooked base. Leave to set.

6 Melt the chocolate in a heatproof bowl over hot water. Spread evenly over the butterscotch layer, then leave to set again before cutting into bars to serve.

> ### cook's tip
> If you prefer you can cook the bars a few days before serving.
> Bake the base on its own, and add the chocolate topping nearer the time.

brioches au chocolat

STEAL OUT OF BED EARLY AND **SURPRISE** SOMEONE **SPECIAL** WITH THESE **WONDERFUL FRENCH** BRIOCHES. LIGHT, GOLDEN AND **DRIZZLED** WITH **MELTED CHOCOLATE**, THEY ARE BOUND TO **GO DOWN WELL**.

method

MAKES 12

1 Sift the flour, salt and sugar into a large bowl and stir in the yeast. Make a well in the centre of the mixture and add the eggs and milk.

2 Beat well, gradually incorporating the surrounding dry ingredients to make a fairly soft dough. Turn on to a lightly floured surface.

3 Knead the dough well until smooth and elastic, adding a little more flour if necessary to prevent the dough becoming soggy.

4 Add the butter to the dough, a few pieces at a time, kneading until each addition is absorbed before adding the next. When all the butter has been incorporated and small bubbles appear in the dough, wrap it and chill for at least 1 hour, or overnight.

5 Lightly grease 12 individual brioche tins set on a baking sheet or a 12-hole brioche or patty tin. Divide the dough into 12 pieces and shape each into a smooth round. Place a chocolate square in the centre. Bring up the sides of the dough and press to seal.

6 Place the brioches, join side down, in the prepared tins. Cover and leave them in a warm place for about 30 minutes, or until doubled in size. Preheat the oven to 200°C/400°F/Gas 6.

7 Brush with beaten egg and bake for 12–15 minutes, until well risen and golden brown. Place on wire racks and leave until cool. Melt the remaining chocolate and drizzle it over the brioches.

ingredients

250g/9oz/2¼ cups **strong white flour**
pinch of **salt**
30ml/2 tbsp **caster sugar**
1 sachet **easy-blend dried yeast**
3 **eggs**, beaten, plus extra beaten **egg**, for glazing
45ml/3 tbsp hand-hot **milk**
115g/4oz/½ cup **unsalted butter**, diced
150g/5oz **plain chocolate**, broken into squares

cook's tip

For the traditional brioche shape, shape three-quarters of the dough into 12 larger balls and the remainder into 12 smaller ones. Put the larger balls in the brioche tins, place the chocolate pieces on them and then top with the smaller balls.

chocolate pecan pie

IF YOU THOUGHT **PECAN PIE** COULDN'T **GET ANY BETTER**, JUST TRY THIS **GORGEOUS** CHOCOLATE VERSION WITH ITS **RICH ORANGE CRUST**.

ingredients

200g/7oz/1¾ cups
  plain flour
65g/2½oz/5 tbsp
  caster sugar
90g/3½oz/scant ½ cup
  unsalted butter, softened
1 **egg**, beaten
finely grated rind of 1 **orange**

For the filling
200g/7oz/¾ cup
  golden syrup
45ml/3 tbsp soft **light muscovado sugar**
150g/5oz **plain chocolate**
  broken into squares
50g/2oz/4 tbsp **butter**
3 **eggs**, beaten
5ml/1 tsp **vanilla essence**
175g/6oz/1½ cups
  pecan nuts

method

SERVES 6

1 Sift the flour into a bowl and stir in the sugar. Work in the butter evenly with the fingertips until combined.

2 Beat the egg and orange rind in a bowl, then stir into the mixture to make a firm dough. Add a little water if the mixture is too dry.

3 Roll out the pastry on a lightly floured surface and use to line a deep, 20cm/8in loose-based flan tin. Chill for 30 minutes.

4 Preheat the oven to 180°C/350°F/Gas 4. Make the filling. Mix the syrup, sugar, chocolate and butter in a small saucepan. Heat gently until melted.

5 Remove from the heat and beat in the eggs and vanilla essence. Sprinkle the pecan nuts into the pastry case and carefully pour over the chocolate mixture.

6 Place on a baking sheet and bake for 50–60 minutes, or until set. Cool in the tin.

---

cook's tip
Although not traditional, this pie would also be delicious made with other kinds of nuts, such as walnut halves.

chocolate frosted fudge cake

RICH AND **DREAMY**, WITH AN **IRRESISTIBLE** CHOCOLATE **FUDGY FROSTING**, THIS CAKE COULDN'T BE **EASIER TO MAKE** OR **MORE WONDERFUL** TO EAT.

ingredients

115g/4oz **plain chocolate**, broken into squares
175g/6oz/3⁄4 cup **unsalted butter** or **margarine**, softened
200g/7oz/generous 1 cup **light muscovado sugar**
5ml/1 tsp **vanilla essence**
3 **eggs**, beaten
150ml/1⁄4 pint/2⁄3 cup **Greek-style yogurt**
150g/5oz/11⁄4 cups **self-raising flour**
icing sugar and **chocolate curls**, to decorate

For the frosting
115g/4oz **plain dark chocolate**, broken into squares
50g/2oz/4 tbsp **unsalted butter**
350g/12oz/3 cups **icing sugar**
90ml/6 tbsp **Greek-style yogurt**

method

SERVES 6–8

1 Preheat the oven to 190°C/375°F/Gas 5. Grease two 20cm/8in round sandwich cake tins and line the base of each with non-stick baking paper. Melt the chocolate in a heatproof bowl over hot water.

2 In a mixing bowl, cream the butter or margarine with the sugar until light and fluffy. Beat in the vanilla essence, then gradually add the beaten eggs, beating well after each addition.

3 Stir in the melted plain chocolate and yogurt evenly. Fold in the flour with a metal spoon.

4 Divide the mixture between the prepared tins. Bake for 25–30 minutes, or until the cakes are firm to the touch. Turn out and cool on a wire rack.

5 Make the frosting. Melt the chocolate and butter in a saucepan over a low heat. Remove from the heat and stir in the icing sugar and yogurt. Mix with a rubber spatula until smooth, then beat until the frosting begins to cool and thicken slightly. Use about a third of the mixture to sandwich the cakes together.

6 Working quickly, spread the remainder over the top and sides. Sprinkle with icing sugar and decorate with chocolate curls.

> ### cook's tip
> If the frosting begins to set too quickly, heat it gently to soften, and beat in a little extra yogurt if necessary.

sticky chocolate, maple & walnut swirls

THIS RICH **YEASTED CAKE** BREAKS INTO SEPARATE **STICKY** CHOCOLATE **SWIRLS**, EACH **SOAKED** IN **MAPLE SYRUP**.

method

MAKES 12

1 Grease a deep 23cm/9in springform cake tin. Sift the flour and cinnamon into a bowl, then rub in the butter until the mixture resembles coarse breadcrumbs.

2 Stir in the sugar and yeast. In a jug or bowl, beat the egg yolk with the water and milk, then stir into the dry ingredients to make a soft dough (see cook's tip).

3 Knead the dough on a lightly floured surface until smooth, then roll out to a rectangle measuring about 40 x 30cm/16 x 12in.

4 For the filling, brush the dough with the melted butter and sprinkle with the sugar, chocolate chips and nuts.

5 Roll up the dough from one long side like a Swiss roll, then cut into 12 thick, even-size slices.

6 Pack the slices closely together in the prepared tin, with the cut sides facing upwards. Cover and leave in a warm place for about 1½ hours, until well risen and springy to the touch. Meanwhile, preheat the oven to 220°C/425°F/Gas 7.

7 Bake the swirls for about 30–35 minutes, until well risen, golden brown and firm. Remove from the tin and place on a wire rack to cool completely. To finish, spoon or brush the maple syrup over the cake. Pull the pieces apart to serve.

ingredients

450g/1lb/4 cups **strong white flour**
2.5ml/½ tsp **ground cinnamon**
50g/2oz/4 tbsp **unsalted butter**
50g/2oz/¼ cup **caster sugar**
1 sachet **easy-blend dried yeast**
1 **egg yolk**
120ml/4fl oz/½ cup **water**
60ml/4 tbsp **milk**
45ml/3 tbsp **maple syrup**,
   to finish

For the filling
40g/1½oz/3 tbsp **unsalted butter**, melted
50g/2oz/⅓ cup **light muscovado sugar**
175g/6oz/1 cup **plain chocolate chips**
75g/3oz/¾ cup chopped **walnuts**

cook's tip
The amount of liquid added to the dry ingredients may have to be adjusted slightly, as some flours absorb more liquid than others. The dough should be soft but not sticky.

ingredients

75g/3oz/¾ cup **plain flour**
45ml/3 tbsp **cocoa powder**
75g/3oz/½ cup **semolina**
50g/2oz/¼ cup **caster sugar**
115g/4oz/½ cup **unsalted butter**, softened

For the filling
225g/8oz/1 cup **cream cheese**
120ml/4fl oz/½ cup **natural yogurt**
2 **eggs**, beaten
75g/3oz/6 tbsp **caster sugar**
finely grated rind of 1 **lemon**
75g/3oz/½ cup **raisins**
45ml/3 tbsp **plain chocolate chips**

For the topping
75g/3oz **plain chocolate**, broken into squares
30ml/2 tbsp **golden syrup**
40g/1½oz/3 tbsp **butter**

baked chocolate & raisin cheesecake

IF YOU JUST **CAN'T GET ENOUGH** CHOCOLATE, THIS **DELECTABLE** CHEESECAKE WILL BE YOUR **IDEA OF HEAVEN**. ITS **CRISP CHOCOLATE** SHORTBREAD BASE IS **SMOTHERED** WITH A **CREAMY** CHOCOLATE CHIP FILLING, **TOPPED** WITH A **STICKY CHOCOLATE** GLAZE.

method

SERVES 8–10

1 Preheat the oven to 150°C/300°F/Gas 2. Sift the flour and cocoa into a mixing bowl and stir in the semolina and sugar. Using your fingertips, work the butter into the flour mixture until it makes a firm dough.

2 Press the dough into the base of a 22cm/8½in springform tin. Prick all over with a fork and bake in the oven for 15 minutes. Remove the tin, but leave the oven on.

3 Make the filling. In a large bowl, beat the cream cheese with the yogurt, eggs and sugar until evenly mixed. Stir in the lemon rind, raisins and chocolate chips.

4 Smooth the cream cheese mixture over the chocolate shortbread base and bake for a further 35–45 minutes, or until the filling is a pale golden colour and just set. Cool in the tin.

5 To make the topping, combine the chocolate, syrup and butter in a heatproof bowl. Set over a saucepan of simmering water and heat gently, stirring occasionally, until melted. Pour over the cheesecake and leave until set.

> ### cook's tip
> For a slightly quicker version, omit the topping and simply drizzle melted chocolate over the cheesecake to finish.

chocolate chip marzipan loaf

SOMETIMES **PLAIN WRAPPERS** DISGUISE THE **MOST MARVELLOUS SURPRISES**. INSIDE THIS ORDINARY-LOOKING LOAF ARE **THICK, CREAMY CHUNKS** OF **MARZIPAN** AND CHIPS OF **CHOCOLATE**.

ingredients

115g/4oz/1/2 cup **unsalted butter**, softened
150g/5oz/scant 1 cup **light muscovado sugar**
2 **eggs**
45ml/3 tbsp **cocoa powder**
150g/5oz/1 1/4 cups **self-raising flour**
130g/4 1/2oz **marzipan**
60ml/4 tbsp **plain chocolate chips**

---

cook's tip

If you have a very sweet tooth, you can substitute milk chocolate chips for the plain ones in this recipe.

---

method

SERVES 6

1 Preheat the oven to 180°C/350°F/Gas 4. Grease a 900g/2lb loaf tin and line the base with non-stick baking paper. Cream the butter and sugar in a mixing bowl until light and fluffy.

2 Add the eggs to the creamed mixture one at a time, beating well after each addition to combine.

3 Sift the cocoa and flour over the mixture and fold in evenly.

4 Chop the marzipan into small pieces with a sharp knife. Tip into a bowl and mix with the chocolate chips. Set aside about 60ml/4 tbsp and fold the rest evenly into the cake mixture.

5 Scrape the mixture into the prepared tin, level the top and scatter with the reserved marzipan and chocolate chips.

6 Bake for 45–50 minutes, or until the loaf is risen and firm. Cool for a few minutes in the tin, then turn out on to a wire rack to cool completely before slicing and serving.

special occasion cakes

death by chocolate

ONE OF THE **RICHEST** CHOCOLATE CAKES EVER, THIS SHOULD BE **SLICED** VERY **THINLY**. **TRUE CHOCOHOLICS** CAN ALWAYS COME BACK **FOR MORE**.

method

SERVES 16–20

1 Preheat the oven to 180°C/350°F/Gas 4. Grease and base-line a deep 23cm/9in springform cake tin. Place the chocolate, butter and milk in a saucepan. Stir over a low heat until smooth. Remove from the heat, beat in the sugar and vanilla, then leave to cool slightly.

2 Beat the egg yolks with cream in a bowl, then beat into the chocolate mixture. Sift the flour and baking powder over the surface and fold in.

3 Whisk the egg whites in a grease-free bowl until stiff; fold into the mixture.

4 Scrape into the prepared tin and bake for about 45–55 minutes, or until firm to the touch. Cool in the tin for 15 minutes, then invert on to a wire rack to cool.

5 Slice the cold cake across the middle to make three even layers. Make the filling. In a small saucepan, warm the jam with 15ml/1 tbsp of the brandy, then brush over two of the layers; leave to set. Place the remaining brandy in a saucepan with the chocolate and butter. Heat gently, stirring, until smooth. Cool until beginning to thicken.

6 Spread the bottom layer of the cake with half the chocolate filling, taking care not to disturb the jam. Top with a second layer, jam side up, and spread with the remaining filling. Top with the final layer and press lightly.

7 Leave to set, then spread the top and sides of the cake with the chocolate ganache. Decorate with chocolate curls and, if liked, chocolate-dipped Cape gooseberries.

> ### cook's tip
> To make chocolate curls, spread a layer of melted chocolate on a firm surface and shave off curls with a knife blade at a 45° angle when set. Chill.

ingredients

225g/8oz **plain dark chocolate**, broken into squares

115g/4oz/1/2 cup **unsalted butter**

150ml/1/4 pint/2/3 cup **milk**

225g/8oz/1 1/4 cups **light muscovado sugar**

10ml/2 tsp **vanilla essence**

2 **eggs**, separated

150ml/1/4 pint/2/3 cup **soured cream**

225g/8oz/2 cups **self-raising flour**

5ml/1 tsp **baking powder**

For the filling and topping

60ml/4 tbsp seedless **raspberry jam**

60ml/4 tbsp **brandy**

400g/14oz **plain dark chocolate**, broken into squares

200g/7oz/scant 1cup **unsalted butter**

1 quantity **Chocolate Ganache**

Cape gooseberries and **chocolate curls**, to decorate

ingredients

6 **eggs**

200g/7oz/scant 1 cup
  caster sugar

5ml/1 tsp **vanilla essence**

50g/2oz/¹⁄2 cup **plain flour**

50g/2oz/¹⁄2 cup
  cocoa powder

115g/4oz/¹⁄2 cup **unsalted
  butter**, melted

For the filling and topping

60ml/4 tbsp **kirsch**

600ml/1 pint/2¹⁄2 cups **double
  or whipping cream**

30ml/2 tbsp **icing sugar**

2.5ml/¹⁄2 tsp **vanilla essence**

675g/1¹⁄2lb jar stoned **morello
  cherries**, drained

To decorate

icing sugar, for dusting

grated chocolate

chocolate curls

fresh or drained canned
  morello cherries

black forest gâteau

THIS **LUSCIOUS** CHOCOLATE SPONGE,
MOISTENED WITH **KIRSCH** AND LAYERED WITH
CHERRIES AND **FRESH CREAM**, IS STILL ONE
OF THE **MOST POPULAR** CHOCOLATE GATEAUX.

method

SERVES 8–10

1 Preheat the oven to 180°C/350°F/Gas 4. Grease three 19cm/7¹⁄2in sandwich cake tins and line the base of each with non-stick baking paper. Whisk the eggs with the sugar and vanilla essence in a bowl until pale and very thick – the mixture should hold a firm trail when the whisk is lifted.

2 Sift the flour and cocoa over the mixture and fold in lightly and evenly. Stir in the melted butter.

3 Divide the mixture among the prepared cake tins, smoothing them level. Bake for 15–18 minutes, until risen and springy to the touch. Leave to cool in the tins for about 5 minutes, then turn out on to wire racks and leave to cool completely.

4 Prick each layer all over with a skewer or fork, then sprinkle with kirsch. Whip the cream in a bowl until it starts to thicken, then beat in the icing sugar and vanilla essence until the mixture begins to hold its shape.

5 To assemble, spread one cake layer with a thick layer of flavoured cream and top with a quarter of the cherries. Spread the second cake layer with cream and cherries, then place it on top of the first layer. Top with the final layer.

6 Spread the remaining cream all over the cake. Dust a plate with icing sugar and position the cake. Press grated chocolate over the sides and decorate with the chocolate curls and cherries.

chocolate coconut roulade

A **RAVISHING ROULADE** TOPPED WITH **CURLS** OF **FRESH COCONUT**, PERFECT FOR THAT **SPECIAL ANNIVERSARY**.

ingredients

150g/5oz/¾ cup
 caster sugar
5 **eggs**, separated
50g/2oz/½ cup
 cocoa powder

For the filling
300ml/½ pint/1¼ cups **double cream**
45ml/3 tbsp **whisky**
50g/2oz piece solid
 creamed coconut
30ml/2 tbsp **caster sugar**

For the topping
coarsely grated curls of
 fresh **coconut**
chocolate curls

method

SERVES 8

1 Preheat the oven to 180°C/350°C/Gas 4. Grease a 32 x 23cm/ 13 x 9in Swiss roll tin. Dust a large sheet of greaseproof paper with 30ml/2 tbsp of the caster sugar.

2 Place the egg yolks in a heatproof bowl. Add the remaining caster sugar and whisk with a hand-held electric mixer until the mixture is thick enough to leave a trail. Sift the cocoa over, then fold in carefully and evenly with a metal spoon.

3 Whisk the egg whites in a clean, grease-free bowl until they form soft peaks. Fold about 15ml/1 tbsp of the whites into the chocolate mixture to lighten it, then fold in the rest evenly.

4 Scrape the mixture into the prepared tin, taking it right into the corners. Smooth the surface with a palette knife, then bake for 20–25 minutes, or until well risen and springy to the touch.

5 Turn the cooked roulade out on to the sugar-dusted greaseproof paper and carefully peel off the lining paper. Cover with a damp, clean dish towel and leave to cool.

6 Make the filling. Whisk the cream with the whisky in a bowl until the mixture just holds its shape, then finely grate the creamed coconut and stir it in with the sugar.

7 Uncover the sponge and spread about three-quarters of the cream mixture to the edges. Roll up carefully from a long side. Transfer to a plate, pipe or spoon the remaining cream mixture on top, then make the coconut curls and place on top with the chocolate curls.

ingredients

115g/4oz/1/2 cup **unsalted butter**, softened
115g/4oz/2/3 cup **dark muscovado sugar**
2 **eggs**
150ml/1/4 pint/2/3 cup **soured cream**
150g/5oz/11/4 cups **self-raising flour**
5ml/1 tsp **baking powder**
45ml/3 tbsp **cocoa powder**
75g/3oz/3/4 cup stemmed **redcurrants**, plus 115g/4oz/ 1 cup **redcurrant sprigs**, to decorate

For the icing
150g/5oz **plain chocolate**, broken into squares
45ml/3 tbsp **redcurrant jelly**
30ml/2 tbsp **dark rum**
120ml/4fl oz/1/2 cup **double cream**

chocolate redcurrant torte

REDCURRANTS ARE **PERFECT PARTNERS** FOR CHOCOLATE IN THIS **GLOSSY** GATEAU. THEIR **SHARP-SWEET** FLAVOUR BALANCES THE RICH CHOCOLATE **BEAUTIFULLY**.

method

SERVES 8–10

1 Preheat the oven to 180°C/350°F/Gas 4. Grease a 1.2 litre/2 pint/ 5 cup ring tin and dust lightly with flour. Cream the butter with the sugar in a mixing bowl until pale and fluffy. Beat in the eggs and soured cream until thoroughly mixed.

2 Sift the flour, baking powder and cocoa over the mixture, then fold in lightly and evenly. Fold in the stemmed redcurrants.

3 Spoon the mixture into the prepared tin and smooth the surface level. Bake for 40–50 minutes, or until well risen and firm. Turn out on to a wire rack and leave to cool completely.

4 Make the icing. Mix the chocolate, redcurrant jelly and rum in a heatproof bowl. Set it over simmering water and heat, stirring occasionally, until the chocolate has melted. Remove from the heat and stir in the cream.

5 Transfer the cooked cake to a serving plate. Spoon the icing evenly over the cake, allowing it to drizzle down the sides. Decorate with redcurrant sprigs just before serving.

---

cook's tip

If redcurrants are not available, use other small soft fruits such as raspberries or blackcurrants instead.

---

caribbean chocolate ring with rum syrup

LAVISH AND **COLOURFUL**, THIS **EXOTIC** CHOCOLATE **GATEAU** CAN BE MADE IN **ADVANCE**, THEN, JUST **BEFORE SERVING**, ADD THE **SYRUP** AND **FRUIT**.

method

SERVES 8–10

1 Preheat the oven to 180°C/350°F/Gas 4. Grease a 1.5 litre/ 2½ pint/6¼ cup ring tin.

2 Cream together the butter and sugar until light and fluffy. Beat in the eggs gradually, beating well, then mix in the bananas, coconut and cream.

3 Sift the flour, cocoa and bicarbonate of soda over the mixture and fold in thoroughly and evenly.

4 Tip into the prepared tin and spread evenly. Bake for 45–50 minutes, until firm to the touch. Cool for about 10 minutes in the tin, then turn out to finish cooling on a wire rack.

5 For the syrup, place the sugar and water in a pan and heat gently until dissolved. Bring to the boil and boil rapidly for 2 minutes. Remove from the heat.

6 Add the rum and chocolate and stir until melted and smooth, then spoon evenly over the cake.

7 Decorate the ring with tropical fruits and chocolate shapes or curls.

> ### cook's tip
> To give the syrup a really good chocolate flavour, use the best quality plain dark chocolate you can find.

ingredients

115g/4oz/½ cup
   unsalted butter
115g/4oz/¾ cup **light muscovado sugar**
2 **eggs**, beaten
2 ripe **bananas**, mashed
30ml/2 tbsp **desiccated coconut**
30ml/2 tbsp **soured cream**
115g/4oz/1 cup **self-raising flour**
2.5ml/½ tsp **bicarbonate of soda**
45ml/3 tbsp **cocoa powder**

For the syrup
115g/4oz/½ cup
   caster sugar
60ml/4 tbsp **water**
30ml/2 tbsp **dark rum**
50g/2oz **plain dark chocolate**, chopped

To decorate
mixture of **tropical fruits**, such as mango, papaya, starfruit and Cape gooseberries
chocolate shapes or **curls**

white cappuccino gâteau

LUSCIOUS, **LAVISH** AND **LACED** WITH **LIQUEUR**, THIS CAKE IS STRICTLY FOR **ADULTS ONLY**.

ingredients

4 **eggs**
115g/4oz/1/2 cup **caster sugar**
15ml/1 tbsp strong **black coffee**
2.5ml/1/2 tsp **vanilla essence**
115g/4oz/1 cup **plain flour**
75g/3oz **white chocolate**,
   coarsely grated

For the filling
120ml/4fl oz/1/2 cup
   double cream
15ml/1 tbsp **coffee liqueur**

For the frosting and topping
15ml/1 tbsp **coffee liqueur**
1 quantity **White Chocolate**
   Frosting
white chocolate curls
cocoa powder or **powdered**
   cinnamon, for dusting

method

1 Preheat the oven to 180°C/350°F/Gas 4. Grease two 19cm/71/2in round sandwich cake tins and line the base of each with non-stick baking paper.

2 Combine the eggs, caster sugar, coffee and vanilla essence in a large heatproof bowl. Place over a saucepan of hot water and whisk until the mixture is pale and thick enough to hold its shape when the whisk is lifted.

3 Sift half the flour over the mixture; fold in gently and evenly. Carefully fold in the remaining flour with the grated white chocolate.

4 Divide the mixture between the prepared tins and smooth level. Bake for 20–25 minutes, until firm and golden brown, then turn out on to wire racks and leave to cool completely.

5 Make the filling. Whip the cream with the coffee liqueur in a bowl until it holds its shape. Spread evenly over one of the cakes, then place the second cake on top.

6 Stir the coffee liqueur into the frosting. Spread over the top and sides of the cake, swirling with a palette knife. Top with curls of white chocolate and dust with cocoa or cinnamon.

> ### cook's tip
> If you don't have any coffee liqueur, use brandy or dark rum instead. For an alcohol-free version, substitute strong black coffee.

ingredients

225g/8oz **plain dark chocolate**,
   broken into squares
150g/5oz/2/3 cup **unsalted**
   butter, softened
115g/4oz/1/2 cup **caster sugar**
8 **eggs**, separated
115g/4oz/1 cup **plain flour**

For the glaze
225g/8oz/1 cup **apricot jam**
15ml/1 tbsp **lemon juice**

For the icing
225g/8oz **plain dark chocolate**,
   broken into squares
200g/7oz/scant 1 cup
   caster sugar
15ml/1 tbsp **golden syrup**
250ml/8fl oz/1 cup
   double cream
5ml/1 tsp **vanilla essence**
plain chocolate curls,
   to decorate

sachertorte

RICH AND **DARK**, WITH A WONDERFUL
FLAVOUR, THIS **GLORIOUS GATEAU** WAS
CREATED IN **VIENNA** IN 1832 BY **FRANZ
SACHER**, CHEF TO THE **IMPERIAL EMPEROR**.

method

SERVES 10–12

1 Preheat the oven to 180°C/350°F/Gas 4. Grease a 23cm/9in round springform cake tin and line with non-stick baking paper. Melt the chocolate in a heatproof bowl over hot water, then remove from the heat.

2 Cream the butter with the sugar in a mixing bowl until pale and fluffy, then add the egg yolks, one at a time, beating after each addition. Beat in the melted chocolate, then sift the flour over the mixture and fold it in evenly.

3 Whisk the egg whites in a clean, grease-free bowl until stiff, then stir about a quarter of the whites into the chocolate mixture to lighten it. Fold in the remaining whites.

4 Tip the mixture into the prepared cake tin and smooth the surface level with the back of a spoon. Bake for about 50–55 minutes, or until firm. Turn out carefully on to a wire rack to cool.

5 Make the glaze. Heat the apricot jam with the lemon juice in a small saucepan until melted, then strain through a sieve into a bowl. Once the cake is cold, slice in half across the middle to make two even-size layers.

6 Brush the top and sides of each layer with the apricot glaze, then sandwich them together. Place on a wire rack.

7 Make the icing. Mix the chocolate, sugar, golden syrup, cream and vanilla essence in a heavy saucepan. Heat gently, stirring constantly, until the mixture is thick and smooth. Simmer gently for 3–4 minutes, without stirring, until the mixture registers 95°C/200°F on a sugar thermometer. Pour the icing quickly over the cake, spreading to cover the top and sides completely. Leave to set, then decorate with chocolate curls. Serve with whipped cream, if wished.

cook's tip
Use the finest dark chocolate you can afford to make this gâteau – the expense will be amply justified when you taste your first mouthful.

rich chocolate leaf gâteau

THICK, **CREAMY** CHOCOLATE GANACHE AND **DARK** AND **WHITE** CHOCOLATE LEAVES **ADORN** THIS **MOUTH-WATERING** GATEAU.

method

SERVES 12–14

1 Preheat the oven to 190°C/375°F/Gas 5. Grease two 22cm/8½in sandwich cake tins and line the base of each with non-stick baking paper. Stir the milk and chocolate over a low heat until the chocolate has melted. Allow to cool slightly.

2 Cream the butter with the sugar in a mixing bowl until pale and fluffy. Beat in the eggs, one at a time, beating well after each addition.

3 Sift the flour and baking powder over the mixture and fold in. Stir in the melted chocolate mixture with the cream, mixing until smooth.

4 Divide between the prepared tins and level the tops. Bake for 30–35 minutes, or until the cakes are well risen and firm to the touch. Cool in the tins for a few minutes, then turn out on to wire racks to cool completely.

5 Sandwich the cake layers together, using all the raspberry conserve.

6 Spread the chocolate ganache over the top and sides of the cake. Swirl the ganache with a knife. Place the cake on a serving plate, and decorate with the dark and white chocolate leaves.

ingredients

150ml/¼ pint/⅔ cup **milk**

75g/3oz **plain dark chocolate**, broken into squares

175g/6oz/¾ cup **unsalted butter**, softened

250g/9oz/1½ cups **light muscovado sugar**

3 **eggs**

250g/9oz/2¼ cups **plain flour**

10ml/2 tsp **baking powder**

75ml/5 tbsp **single cream**

For the filling and topping

60ml/4 tbsp **raspberry conserve**

1 quantity **Chocolate Ganache**

dark and white **chocolate leaves**

cook's tip
Make a mixture of dark, milk and white chocolate leaves, or marble the mixtures for a variegated effect. Prepare the chocolate leaves in advance to save time, and store them in a covered container in a cool, dry place.

meringue pyramid

ROSES SPELL **ROMANCE** FOR THIS **IMPRESSIVE** CAKE. IT MAKES THE **PERFECT CENTREPIECE** FOR A **CELEBRATION** BUFFET TABLE, AND MOST OF THE **PREPARATION** CAN BE DONE **IN ADVANCE**.

ingredients

4 **egg whites**

pinch of **salt**

175g/6oz/3/4 cup
   caster sugar

5ml/1 tsp **ground cinnamon**

75g/3oz **plain dark
   chocolate**, grated

icing sugar and fresh **rose
   petals**, to decorate

For the filling

115g/4oz **plain chocolate**,
   broken into squares

5ml/1 tsp **vanilla essence**
   or **rose water**

115g/4oz/1/2 cup **mascarpone
   cheese**

method

SERVES 6–8

1 Preheat the oven to 150°C/300°F/Gas 2. Line two large baking sheets with non-stick baking paper. Whisk the egg whites with the salt in a clean, grease-free bowl until they form stiff peaks.

2 Gradually whisk in half the sugar, then add the rest and whisk until the meringue is very stiff and glossy. Add the cinnamon and chocolate and whisk lightly to mix.

3 Draw a 20cm/8in circle on the lining paper on one of the baking sheets, replace it upside down, and spread the marked circle evenly with about half the meringue. Spoon the remaining meringue in 28–30 small neat heaps on both baking sheets. Bake for 1–1½ hours, or until crisp.

4 Make the filling. Melt the chocolate in a heatproof bowl over hot water. Cool slightly, then add the vanilla essence or rose water and cheese. Cool the mixture until it holds its shape.

5 Spoon the chocolate mixture into a large piping bag and sandwich the small meringues together in pairs, reserving a small amount of filling for the pyramid.

6 Arrange the filled meringues on a serving platter, piling them up in a pyramid and keeping them in position with a few well-placed dabs of the reserved filling. Dust the pyramid with icing sugar, sprinkle with the rose petals and serve.

> ### cook's tip
> The meringues can be made up to a week in advance and stored in an airtight container in a cool, dry place.

ingredients

225g/8oz **plain dark chocolate**,
  broken into squares
225g/8oz/1 cup **unsalted
  butter**, softened
200g/7oz/generous 1 cup **dark
  muscovado sugar**
6 **eggs**, separated
5ml/1 tsp **vanilla essence**
150g/5oz/1¼ cups
  ground hazelnuts
60ml/4 tbsp fresh
  white breadcrumbs
finely grated rind of 1 large **orange**
1 quantity **Chocolate Ganache**,
  for filling and frosting
icing sugar, for dusting

For the brandy snaps
50g/2oz/4 tbsp **unsalted butter**
50g/2oz/¼ cup **caster sugar**
75g/3oz/⅓ cup **golden syrup**
50g/2oz/½ cup **plain flour**
5ml/1 tsp **brandy**

chocolate brandy snap gâteau

TAKE YOUR **PLEASURE** SLOWLY BY
SAVOURING **EVERY MOUTHFUL** OF THIS
SENSATIONAL DARK CHOCOLATE GATEAU,
TOPPED WITH **BRANDY SNAP** FRILLS.

method
SERVES 8

1 Preheat the oven to 180°C/350°F/Gas 4. Grease two 20cm/8in sandwich cake tins and line the base of each with non-stick baking paper. Melt the chocolate in a heatproof bowl over hot water. Remove from the heat.

2 Cream the butter with the sugar in a bowl until pale and fluffy. Beat in the egg yolks and vanilla essence. Stir in the chocolate.

3 In a clean, grease-free bowl, whisk the egg whites to soft peaks, then fold them into the chocolate mixture with the ground hazelnuts, breadcrumbs and orange rind.

4 Divide the cake mixture between the prepared tins and smooth the tops. Bake for 25–30 minutes, or until well risen and firm. Turn out on to wire racks.

5 Make the brandy snaps. Line two baking sheets with non-stick baking paper. Heat the butter, sugar and syrup in a saucepan over a gentle heat, stirring occasionally until smooth. Remove from the heat and stir in the flour and brandy.

6 Place small spoonfuls well apart on the baking sheets and bake for 10–15 minutes, until golden. Cool for a few seconds until firm enough to lift on to a wire rack.

7 Immediately pinch the edges of each brandy snap to make a frilled effect. If the biscuits become too firm, pop them back into the oven for a few minutes. Leave to set.

8 Sandwich the cake layers together with half the chocolate ganache, transfer to a plate and spread the remaining ganache on top.

9 Arrange the brandy snap frills over the gâteau and dust with icing sugar.

strawberry chocolate valentine gâteau

OFFERING **A SLICE** OF THIS **VOLUPTUOUS VALENTINE** GATEAU COULD BE THE START OF A LONG AND **VERY SPECIAL ROMANCE**.

method

SERVES 12–14

1 Preheat the oven to 160°C/325°F/Gas 3. Grease a deep 20cm/8in heart-shaped cake tin and line the base with non-stick baking paper. Sift the flour, baking powder and cocoa into a mixing bowl. Stir in the sugar, then make a well in the centre.

2 Add the eggs, treacle, oil and milk to the well. Mix with a spoon to incorporate the dry ingredients, then beat with a hand-held electric mixer until the mixture is smooth and creamy.

3 Spoon the mixture into the prepared cake tin and spread evenly. Bake for about 45 minutes, until well risen and firm to the touch. Cool in the tin for a few minutes, then turn out on to a wire rack to cool completely.

4 Using a sharp knife, slice the cake neatly into two layers. Place the bottom layer on a board or plate. Spread with strawberry jam.

5 Whip the cream in a bowl until it holds its shape. Stir in the strawberries, then spread over the jam. Top with the remaining cake layer.

6 Roll out the chocolate fondant and cover the cake. Decorate with chocolate hearts and dust with icing sugar.

ingredients

175g/6oz/1½ cups **self-raising flour**
10ml/2 tsp **baking powder**
75ml/5 tbsp **cocoa powder**
115g/4oz/½ cup **caster sugar**
2 **eggs**, beaten
15ml/1 tbsp **black treacle**
150ml/¼ pint/⅔ cup **sunflower oil**
150ml/¼ pint/⅔ cup **milk**

For the filling
45ml/3 tbsp **strawberry jam**
150ml/¼ pint/⅔ cup **double** or **whipping cream**
115g/4oz **strawberries**, sliced

To decorate
1 quantity **Chocolate Fondant**
chocolate hearts
icing sugar, for dusting

cook's tip
Keep the fondant closely covered until you are ready to use it, as the surface dries out fairly quickly. If this happens, the smooth effect will be spoiled.

hot puddings

chocolate chip & banana pudding

HOT AND **STEAMY**, THIS **SUPERB LIGHT** PUDDING HAS A **TOTALLY BEGUILING BANANA** AND **CHOCOLATE** FLAVOUR.

method

SERVES 4

1 Prepare a steamer or half fill a saucepan with water and bring it to the boil. Grease a 1litre/1¾ pint/4 cup pudding basin. Sift the flour into a bowl and rub in the unsalted butter or margarine until the mixture resembles coarse breadcrumbs.

2 Mash the bananas in a bowl. Stir them into the creamed mixture, with the caster sugar.

3 Whisk the milk with the egg in a jug or bowl, then beat into the pudding mixture. Stir in the chocolate chips or chopped chocolate.

4 Spoon the mixture into the prepared basin, cover closely with a double thickness of foil and steam for 2 hours, topping up the water as required during cooking.

5 Run a knife around the top of the pudding to loosen it, then turn it out on to a serving dish. Serve hot, with the chocolate sauce.

cook's tip
If you have a food processor, make a quick-mix version by processing all the ingredients, except the chocolate, until smooth. Stir in the chocolate and proceed as in the recipe.

ingredients

200g/7oz/1¾ cups **self-raising flour**
75g/3oz/6 tbsp **unsalted butter** or **margarine**
2 ripe **bananas**
75g/3oz/⅓ cup **caster sugar**
60ml/4 tbsp **milk**
1 **egg**, beaten
60ml/4 tbsp **plain chocolate chips** or chopped **plain chocolate**
Glossy Chocolate Sauce, to serve

ingredients

50g/2oz/4 tbsp **butter**

200g/7oz/generous 1cup **light muscovado sugar**

475ml/16fl oz/2 cups **milk**

90g/3½oz/scant 1cup **self-raising flour**

5ml/1 tsp **ground cinnamon**

75ml/5 tbsp **cocoa powder**

Greek-style yogurt or **vanilla ice cream**, to serve

magic chocolate mud pudding

A **POPULAR** FAVOURITE, WHICH **MAGICALLY SEPARATES** INTO A **LIGHT** AND **AIRY** SPONGE **TOP LAYER** OVER A **SMOOTH** AND **VELVETY** CHOCOLATE SAUCE.

method   SERVES 4

1 Preheat the oven to 180°C/350°F/Gas 4. Lightly grease a 1.5 litre/2½ pint/6 cup ovenproof dish and place on a baking sheet.

2 Place the butter in a saucepan. Add 115g/4oz/¾ cup of the sugar and 150ml/¼ pint/⅔ cup of the milk. Heat gently, stirring from time to time, until the butter has melted and all the sugar has dissolved. Remove the pan from the heat.

3 Sift the flour, cinnamon and 15 ml/1 tbsp of the cocoa powder into the pan and stir into the mixture, mixing evenly. Pour the mixture into the prepared dish and level the surface.

4 Sift the remaining sugar and cocoa powder into a bowl, mix well, then sprinkle over the pudding mixture.

5 Pour the remaining milk over the pudding.

6 Bake for 45–50 minutes, or until the sponge has risen to the top and is firm to the touch. Serve hot, with the yogurt or ice cream.

cook's tip
A soufflé dish or similar straight-sided ovenproof dish is ideal for this, since it supports the sponge as it rises above the sauce.

peachy chocolate bake

RESIST EVERYTHING EXCEPT **TEMPTATION**, SAID OSCAR WILDE.
NEXT TIME YOU **CRAVE** SOMETHING **HOT** AND **CHOCOLATEY**, RAID
THE STORE CUPBOARD AND **WHIP UP** THIS **DELICIOUS PUDDING**.

ingredients

200g/7oz **plain dark chocolate**,
  broken into squares
115g/4oz/1/2 cup
  unsalted butter
4 **eggs**, separated
115g/4oz/1/2 cup
  caster sugar
425g/15oz can **peach
  slices**, drained
whipped cream or **crème
  fraîche**, to serve

method

SERVES 6

1 Preheat the oven to 160°C/325°F/Gas 3. Butter a wide ovenproof
  dish. Melt the chocolate with the butter in a heatproof bowl set over
  a pan of simmering water. Remove from the heat.

2 In a bowl, whisk the egg yolks with the sugar until thick and pale.
  In a clean, grease-free bowl, whisk the whites until stiff.

3 Beat the melted chocolate into the egg yolk mixture.

4 Fold the whites lightly and evenly into the mixture in the bowl.

5 Fold the peach slices into the mixture, then tip into the prepared dish.

6 Bake for 35–40 minutes, or until risen and just firm. Serve the
  pudding hot, with whipped cream or crème fraîche, if you like.

---

cook's tip
Don't level the mixture in the dish before baking. It looks more interesting if the
surface is left rough and uneven.

ingredients

25g/1oz/2 tbsp **unsalted butter**,
  melted

65g/2½oz/generous ½ cup
  cocoa powder

75g/3oz/⅓ cup **caster sugar**

60ml/4 tbsp strong
  black coffee

30ml/2 tbsp **dark rum**

6 **egg whites**

icing sugar, for dusting

---

cook's tip

To serve the soufflés at a dinner
party, prepare them just before the
meal is served. Pop them in the oven
as soon as the main course is
finished and serve freshly baked.

hot mocha rum soufflés

THESE **SUPERB SOUFFLÉS** WILL **ALWAYS RISE** TO **THE OCCASION**. SERVE THEM STRAIGHT FROM THE OVEN FOR A **DECADENT FINALE** TO A DINNER PARTY.

method

SERVES 6

1 Preheat the oven with a baking sheet inside to 190°C/375°F/Gas 5. Grease six 250ml/8fl oz/1 cup soufflé dishes with melted butter.

2 Mix 15ml/1 tbsp of the cocoa with 15ml/1 tbsp of the caster sugar in a bowl. Tip the mixture into each of the dishes in turn, rotating them so that they are evenly coated.

3 Mix the remaining cocoa with the coffee and rum.

4 Whisk the egg whites in a clean, grease-free bowl until they form firm peaks. Whisk in the remaining caster sugar. Stir a generous spoonful of the whites into the cocoa mixture to lighten it, then fold in the remaining whites.

5 Spoon the mixture into the prepared dishes, using the back of the spoon to smooth the tops. Place the dishes on the hot baking sheet and bake for 12–15 minutes, or until well risen. Serve immediately, lightly dusted with icing sugar.

steamed chocolate & fruit puddings

DARK, **FLUFFY** CHOCOLATE SPONGE IS TOPPED WITH **TANGY CRANBERRIES** AND **APPLE**, AND SERVED WITH A **HONEYED** CHOCOLATE **SYRUP**.

method

SERVES 4

1 Prepare a steamer or half fill a saucepan with water and bring it to the boil. Grease four individual pudding basins and sprinkle each one with a little of the muscovado sugar to coat well all over.

2 Peel and core the apple. Dice it into a bowl, add the cranberries and mix well. Divide among the prepared pudding basins.

3 Place the remaining muscovado sugar in a mixing bowl. Add the margarine, eggs, flour, baking powder and cocoa; beat until combined and smooth.

4 Spoon the mixture into the basins and cover each with a double thickness of foil. Steam for about 45 minutes, topping up the boiling water as required, until the puddings are well risen and firm.

5 Make the syrup. Mix the chocolate, honey, butter and vanilla essence in a small saucepan. Heat gently, stirring, until melted and smooth.

6 Run a knife around the edge of each pudding to loosen it, then turn out on to individual plates. Serve at once, with the chocolate syrup.

ingredients

115g/4oz/²⁄₃ cup **dark muscovado sugar**
1 **eating apple**
75g/3oz/¾ cup **cranberries**, thawed if frozen
115g/4oz/½ cup soft **margarine**
2 **eggs**
75g/3oz/¾ cup **plain flour**
2.5ml/½ tsp **baking powder**
45ml/3 tbsp **cocoa powder**

For the chocolate syrup
115g/4oz **plain chocolate**, broken into squares
30ml/2 tbsp **clear honey**
15ml/1 tbsp **unsalted butter**
2.5ml/½ tsp **vanilla essence**

cook's tip
The puddings can be cooked very quickly in the microwave. Use non-metallic basins and cover with greaseproof paper instead of foil. Cook at 100% Full Power for 5–6 minutes, then leave to stand for 2–3 minutes before turning out.

chocolate, date & almond filo coil

EXPERIENCE THE **ALLURE** OF THE **MIDDLE EAST** WITH THIS DELECTABLE DESSERT. **CRISP FILO** PASTRY **CONCEALS** A **CHOCOLATE** AND **ROSE WATER** FILLING, **STUDDED** WITH DATES AND ALMONDS.

ingredients

275g/10oz packet **filo pastry**, thawed if frozen

50g/2oz/4 tbsp **unsalted butter**, melted

icing sugar, cocoa powder and **ground cinnamon**, for dusting

For the filling

75g/3oz/6 tbsp **unsalted butter**

115g/4oz **plain dark chocolate**, broken into squares

115g/4oz/1 cup **ground almonds**

115g/4oz/2/3 cup chopped **dates**

75g/3oz/2/3 cup **icing sugar**

10ml/2 tsp **rose water**

2.5ml/1/2 tsp **ground cinnamon**

method

SERVES 6

1 Preheat the oven to 180°C/350°F/Gas 4. Grease a 22cm/8½in round cake tin. Make the filling. Melt the butter with the chocolate in a heatproof bowl over barely simmering water, then remove from the heat and stir in the remaining ingredients to make a thick paste. Leave to cool.

2 Lay one sheet of filo on a clean work surface (see cook's tip). Brush it with melted butter, then lay a second sheet on top and brush with melted butter.

3 Roll a handful of the chocolate almond mixture into a long sausage shape and place along one long edge of the layered filo. Roll the pastry tightly around the filling to make a roll.

4 Place the roll around the outside of the tin. Make enough rolls to fill the tin.

5 Brush the coil with the remaining melted butter, then bake for 30–35 minutes, until the pastry is golden brown and crisp. Remove the coil from the tin; place it on a plate. Serve warm, dusted with icing sugar, cocoa and cinnamon.

---

cook's tip
Filo pastry dries out very quickly, so remove one sheet at a time and keep the rest covered with a slightly damp, clean dish towel.

pears in chocolate fudge blankets

WARM **POACHED** PEARS **SWATHED** IN A RICH CHOCOLATE **FUDGE SAUCE** – WHO COULD **RESIST** SUCH A **SENSUAL PLEASURE**?

method

SERVES 6

1 Peel the pears thinly, leaving the stalks on. Scoop out the cores from the base. Brush the cut surfaces with lemon juice to prevent browning.

2 Place the sugar and water in a large saucepan. Heat gently until the sugar dissolves. Add the pears and cinnamon stick with any remaining lemon juice, and, if necessary a little more water, to cover the pears.

3 Bring to the boil, then lower the heat, cover the pan and simmer the pears gently for 15–20 minutes, or until they are just tender.

4 Meanwhile, make the sauce. Place the cream, sugar, butter, golden syrup and milk in a heavy-based saucepan. Heat gently until the sugar has dissolved and the butter and syrup have melted, then bring to the boil. Boil, stirring constantly, for about 5 minutes or until the sauce is thick and smooth. Remove from the heat and stir in the chocolate, a few squares at a time, until melted.

5 Using a slotted spoon, transfer the poached pears to a dish. Keep hot. Boil the syrup rapidly to reduce to about 45–60ml/3–4 tbsp. Remove the cinnamon stick and stir the syrup into the chocolate sauce.

6 Serve the pears on individual dessert plates, with the hot chocolate fudge sauce spooned over.

ingredients

6 ripe **eating pears**
30ml/2 tbsp **lemon juice**
75g/3oz/1/3 cup **caster sugar**
300ml/1/2 pint/11/4 cups **water**
1 **cinnamon stick**

For the sauce
200ml/7fl oz/scant 1 cup **double cream**
150g/5oz/scant 1 cup **light muscovado sugar**
25g/1oz/2 tbsp **unsalted butter**
60ml/4 tbsp **golden syrup**
120ml/4fl oz/1/2 cup **milk**
200g/7oz **plain dark chocolate**, broken into squares

ingredients

6 **egg yolks**

150g/5oz/⅔ cup **caster sugar**

45ml/3 tbsp **cocoa powder**

200ml/7fl oz/scant 1cup **Marsala**

cocoa powder or **icing sugar**,
  for dusting

hot chocolate zabaglione

ONCE YOU'VE **TASTED** THIS **SLINKY**, **SENSUOUS** DESSERT, YOU'LL **NEVER LOOK** AT COCOA IN **QUITE** THE **SAME WAY** AGAIN.

method

SERVES 6

1 Half fill a medium saucepan with water and bring to simmering point. Select a heatproof bowl which will fit over the pan, making sure that the base of the bowl does not touch the surface of the water. Away from the heat, place the egg yolks and sugar in the bowl and whisk until the mixture is pale and all the sugar has dissolved.

2 Add the cocoa and Marsala, then place the bowl over the simmering water. Whisk with a hand-held electric mixer until the mixture is smooth, thick and foamy.

3 Pour quickly into tall heatproof glasses, dust lightly with cocoa or icing sugar and serve immediately, with chocolate cinnamon tuiles or amaretti biscuits.

cook's tip
Zabaglione must be served as soon as it is ready. For a dinner party, assemble all the equipment and ingredients ahead of time, so that all you have to do is quickly mix everything together as soon as the main course is over.

chocolate crêpes with plums & port

A **WONDERFUL** DESSERT FOR A **SPECIAL DINNER**, THIS DISH CAN BE MADE **IN ADVANCE** AND ALWAYS **LOOKS IMPRESSIVE**.

ingredients

50g/2oz **plain chocolate**,
broken into squares
200ml/7fl oz/scant 1 cup **milk**
120ml/4fl oz/1/2 cup
 single cream
30ml/2 tbsp **cocoa powder**
115g/4oz/1 cup **plain flour**
2 **eggs**

For the filling
500g/11/4lb red or golden **plums**
50g/2oz/1/4 cup **caster sugar**
30ml/2 tbsp **water**
30ml/2 tbsp **port**
oil, for frying
175g/6oz/3/4 cup
 crème fraîche

For the sauce
150g/5oz **plain chocolate**,
broken into squares
175ml/6fl oz/3/4 cup
 double cream
30ml/2 tbsp **port**

method

SERVES 6

1 Place the chocolate in a saucepan with the milk. Heat gently until the chocolate has melted. Pour into a blender or food processor and add the cream, cocoa powder, flour and eggs. Process until smooth, then tip into a jug and chill for 30 minutes.

2 Meanwhile, make the filling. Halve and stone the plums. Place them in a saucepan and add the sugar and water. Bring to the boil, then lower the heat, cover, and simmer for about 10 minutes, or until the plums are tender. Stir in the port and simmer for a further 30 seconds. Remove from the heat and keep warm.

3 Have ready a sheet of non-stick baking paper. Heat a crêpe pan, grease it lightly with a little oil, then pour in just enough batter to cover the base of the pan, swirling to coat evenly. Cook until the crêpe has set, then flip it over to cook the other side. Slide the crêpe out on to the sheet of paper, then cook 9–11 more crêpes in the same way.

4 Make the sauce. Combine the chocolate and cream in a saucepan. Heat gently, stirring until smooth. Add the port and continue to heat the sauce for about 1 minute, stirring all the time.

5 Divide the plum filling between the crêpes, add a dollop of crème fraîche to each and roll them up carefully. Serve on individual dessert plates, with the chocolate sauce spooned generously over the top.

---

cook's tip
Vary the fruit according to what is in season, using a complementary liqueur or spirit. Try cherries with Kirsch or cherry brandy, mandarin orange segments with Grand Marnier or Cointreau or poached pears or apples with Calvados. All will taste wonderful with chocolate.

chocolate & orange pancakes

FLIP FOR THESE **FABULOUS** BABY **PANCAKES** IN A RICH CREAMY **ORANGE LIQUEUR** SAUCE. SERVE THEM **STRAIGHT** FROM THE **PAN** TO **ENJOY** THEM AT THEIR **BEST**.

ingredients

method

SERVES 4

115g/4oz/1 cup **self-raising flour**
30ml/2 tbsp **cocoa powder**
2 **eggs**
50g/2oz **plain chocolate**, broken into squares
200ml/7fl oz/scant 1 cup **milk**
finely grated rind of 1 **orange**
30ml/2 tbsp **orange juice**
butter or **oil**, for frying
60ml/4 tbsp **chocolate curls**, for sprinkling

For the sauce
2 large **oranges**
30ml/2 tbsp **unsalted butter**
45ml/3 tbsp **light muscovado sugar**
250ml/8fl oz/1 cup **crème fraîche**
30ml/2 tbsp **Grand Marnier** or **Cointreau**
chocolate curls, to decorate

1 Sift the flour and cocoa into a bowl and make a well in the centre. Add the eggs and beat well, gradually incorporating the surrounding dry ingredients to make a smooth batter.

2 Mix the chocolate and milk in a saucepan. Heat gently until the chocolate has melted, then beat into the batter until smooth and bubbly. Stir in the orange rind and juice.

3 Heat a large heavy-based frying pan or griddle. Grease with a little butter or oil. Drop large spoonfuls of batter on to the hot surface, leaving room for spreading. Cook over a moderate heat. When the pancakes are lightly browned underneath and bubbly on top, flip them over to cook the other side. Slide on to a plate and keep warm, then make more in the same way.

4 Make the sauce. Grate the rind of 1 orange into a bowl and set aside. Peel both oranges, taking care to remove all the pith, then slice the flesh fairly thinly.

5 Heat the butter and sugar in a wide, shallow pan over a low heat, stirring constantly until the sugar has dissolved. Stir in the crème fraîche and heat gently.

6 Add the pancakes and orange slices to the sauce, heat gently for 1–2 minutes. Spoon the orange liqueur over the pancakes and sprinkle with the reserved orange rind. Scatter over the chocolate curls and serve.

---

cook's tip
Use the finest dark chocolate you can afford to make these pancakes, to counterbalance the rich orange liqueur sauce.

cold desserts

tiramisu in chocolate cups

GIVE IN TO THE **TEMPTATION** OF TIRAMISU, WITH ITS **MAGICAL MOCHA** FLAVOUR.

method

SERVES 6

1 Make the chocolate cups. Cut out six 15cm/6in rounds of non-stick baking paper. Melt the chocolate with the butter in a heatproof bowl set over a pan of barely simmering water. Stir until smooth, then spread a spoonful of the chocolate mixture over each baking paper round, to within 2cm/¾in of the edge.

2 Carefully lift each paper round and drape it over an upturned teacup or ramekin so that the edges curve into frills. Leave until completely set, then carefully lift off and peel away the paper to reveal the chocolate cups.

3 Make the filling. Beat the egg yolk and sugar in a bowl until smooth, then stir in the vanilla essence and mascarpone. Mix to a smooth creamy consistency.

4 In a separate bowl, mix the coffee, cocoa and liqueur. Break up the biscuits roughly and stir them into the mixture.

5 Place the chocolate cups on individual plates. Divide half the biscuit mixture among them, then spoon over half the mascarpone mixture.

6 Spoon over the remaining biscuit mixture, top with the rest of the mascarpone mixture and dust with cocoa. Serve as soon as possible.

ingredients

1 **egg yolk**
30ml/2 tbsp **caster sugar**
2.5ml/½ tsp **vanilla essence**
250g/9oz/generous 1 cup
   mascarpone cheese
120ml/4fl oz/½ cup strong
   black coffee
15ml/1 tbsp **cocoa powder**
30ml/2 tbsp **coffee liqueur**
16 **amaretti biscuits**
cocoa powder, for dusting

For the chocolate cups
175g/6oz **plain chocolate**,
   broken into squares
25g/1oz/2 tbsp **unsalted butter**

cook's tip
When spreading the chocolate for the cups, don't aim for perfectly regular edges; uneven edges will give a more frilled effect.

ingredients

65g/2½oz/5 tbsp **unsalted butter**
250g/9oz **milk chocolate digestive biscuits**
chocolate curls, to decorate

For the filling
397g/13oz can **condensed milk**
150g/5oz **plain chocolate**, broken into squares
120ml/4fl oz/½ cup **crème fraîche** or **single cream**
15ml/1 tbsp **golden syrup**

For the topping
2 **bananas**
250ml/8fl oz/1 cup **crème fraîche**
10ml/2 tbsp strong **black coffee**

chocolate, banana & toffee pie

CHOCOHOLICS LOVE FINDING **NEW WAYS** OF USING THEIR **FAVOURITE INGREDIENT**. HERE'S HOW IT CAN **HELP** TO MAKE THE FAMOUS **BANOFFEE** PIE **EVEN MORE DELICIOUS**.

method   SERVES 6

1 Melt the unsalted butter in a saucepan. Crush the biscuits quite finely in a food processor or with a rolling pin. Place them in a bowl and stir in the hot melted butter. Press them on to the base and sides of a 23cm/9in loose-based flan tin. Leave to set.

2 Make the filling. Place the unopened can of condensed milk in a saucepan of boiling water and cover with a lid. Lower the heat and simmer for 2 hours, topping up the water as necessary. Do not allow to boil dry.

3 Remove the pan from the heat and set aside, covered, until the can has cooled down completely in the water. Do not attempt to open the can until it is completely cold, as the contents will be under pressure due to the heat.

4 Melt the chocolate with the crème fraîche or single cream and golden syrup in a heatproof bowl over barely simmering water. Stir in the caramelized condensed milk and beat until evenly mixed, then spread the filling over the biscuit crust.

5 Slice the bananas and arrange them over the chocolate filling.

6 Stir together the crème fraîche and coffee, then spoon over the bananas. Decorate liberally with the chocolate curls.

rich chocolate sorbet with redcurrants

CHOCOLATE SORBET IS THE **CHILL** THAT **THRILLS**. FOR A REALLY **FINE TEXTURE**, AN **ICE CREAM** MAKER WILL **CHURN** THE MIXTURE AS IT **FREEZES**, BUT YOU CAN ALSO MAKE IT **BY HAND** VERY EASILY.

ingredients

475ml/16fl oz/2 cups **water**

45ml/3 tbsp **clear honey**

115g/4oz/1/2 cup **caster sugar**

75g/3oz/3/4 cup **cocoa powder**

50g/2oz **plain dark chocolate**, broken into squares

400g/14oz **redcurrants** or other **soft red fruits**, such as raspberries or strawberries

cook's tip

To serve the sorbet in neat oval scoops, use a tablespoon to take a scoop out of the sorbet, then use another tablespoon to smooth it off and transfer it to the plate. Rinsing the spoons in hot water before use will give the scoops a cleaner shape.

method

SERVES 6

1 Place the water, honey, sugar and cocoa in a saucepan. Heat gently, stirring occasionally, until the sugar has completely dissolved.

2 Remove from the heat, add the chocolate and stir until melted. Leave until cool.

3 Tip into an ice cream maker and churn until frozen. Alternatively, pour into a container suitable for use in the freezer, freeze until slushy, whisk until smooth, then freeze again. Whisk for a second time before the mixture hardens completely.

4 Remove from the freezer 10–15 minutes before serving, so that the sorbet softens slightly. Serve in scoops, with the soft fruits.

PURE LUXURY – EXOTIC FRUIT IN A **THICK**, **HONEYED CHOCOLATE CUSTARD**, TOPPED WITH A **CRUNCHY COATING** OF CARAMELIZED SUGAR.

ingredients

2 ripe **mangoes**

300ml/½ pint/1¼ cups
   double cream

300ml/½ pint/1¼ cups
   crème fraîche

1 **vanilla pod**

115g/4oz **plain dark**
   chocolate, broken into squares

4 **egg yolks**

15ml/1 tbsp **clear honey**

90ml/6 tbsp **demerara sugar**,
   for the topping

mango & chocolate crème brûlée

method

SERVES 6

1 Halve, stone and peel the mangoes. Roughly chop the flesh and divide it among six individual flameproof dishes set on a baking sheet.

2 Mix the double cream and crème fraîche in a large heatproof bowl and add the vanilla pod. Place the bowl over a saucepan of barely simmering water and stir for about 10 minutes. Do not let the bowl touch the water or the cream may overheat.

3 Remove the vanilla pod and stir in the chocolate, a few pieces at a time, until melted. When the mixture is completely smooth, remove the bowl, but leave the pan of water over the heat.

4 Whisk the egg yolks and clear honey in a second heatproof bowl, then gradually pour in the chocolate cream, whisking constantly. Place over the pan of barely simmering water and stir until the chocolate custard thickens enough to coat the back of a wooden spoon.

5 Remove the bowl from the heat and spoon the custard over the mangoes. Cool, then chill until set.

6 Preheat the grill to high. Sprinkle 15ml/1 tbsp demerara sugar evenly over each dessert and spray lightly with a little water. Grill briefly, as close to the heat as possible, until the sugar melts and caramelizes. Chill again before serving the desserts.

cook's tip
The mango and chocolate custard base can be prepared up to two days in advance. Make the caramelized sugar topping several hours before serving so that the desserts can be chilled.

chocolate & hazelnut galettes

THERE IS **STACKS** OF **SOPHISTICATION** IN THESE **TRIPLE-TIERED** CHOCOLATE ROUNDS, SANDWICHED **TOGETHER** WITH A **LIGHT FROMAGE FRAIS** FILLING.

method

SERVES 4

1 Melt the squares of plain chocolate in a heatproof bowl set over a pan of barely simmering water. Remove the bowl from the heat and stir the single cream into the chocolate.

ingredients

175g/6oz **plain chocolate**,
   broken into squares
45ml/3 tbsp **single cream**
30ml/2 tbsp **flaked hazelnuts**
115g/4oz **white chocolate**,
   broken into squares
175g/6oz/3/4 cup **fromage frais**
15ml/1 tbsp **dry sherry**
60ml/4 tbsp finely chopped
   hazelnuts, toasted
Cape gooseberries, dipped in
   white chocolate, to decorate

---

cook's tip
The chocolate could be spread over heart shapes instead of rounds, if you like, for a Valentine's Day dessert.

---

2 Draw 12 x 7.5cm/3in circles on sheets of non-stick baking paper. Turn the paper over and spread the plain chocolate over each marked circle, covering in a thin, even layer. Scatter flaked hazelnuts over four of the circles, then leave until set.

3 Melt the white chocolate in a heatproof bowl over hot water, then stir in the fromage frais and dry sherry. Fold in the chopped, toasted hazelnuts. Leave to cool until the mixture holds its shape.

4 Remove the plain chocolate rounds carefully from the paper and sandwich them together in stacks of three, spooning the white chocolate hazelnut cream between each layer and using the hazelnut-covered rounds on top. Chill before serving.

5 To serve, place the galettes on individual plates and decorate with chocolate-dipped Cape gooseberries.

white chocolate vanilla mousse

HAPPY ENDINGS ARE **ASSURED** WHEN SLICES OF THIS **CREAMY WHITE** CHOCOLATE **MOUSSE** ARE SERVED WITH A **TRULY DIVINE** DARK **SAUCE**.

ingredients

200g/7oz **white chocolate**, broken into squares
2 **eggs**, separated
60ml/4 tbsp **caster sugar**
300ml/1/2 pint/11/4 cups **double cream**
1 sachet powdered **gelatine**
150ml/1/4 pint/2/3 cup **Greek-style yogurt**
10ml/2 tsp **vanilla essence**

For the sauce
50g/2oz **plain chocolate**, broken into squares
30ml/2 tbsp **dark rum**
60ml/4 tbsp **single cream**

cook's tip
It is very important to make sure that the gelatine is completely dissolved in the cream before adding to the other ingredients. Lift a little of the mixture on a wooden spoon to check that no undissolved granules remain. Alternatively, soften the gelatine in 30ml/2 tbsp cold water in a cup, then melt it over hot water before stirring it into the heated cream.

method

SERVES 6–8

1 Line a 1 litre/13/4 pint/4 cup loaf tin with non-stick baking paper or clear film. Melt the chocolate in a heatproof bowl over hot water, then remove from the heat.

2 Whisk the egg yolks and sugar in a bowl until pale and thick, then beat in the melted chocolate.

3 Heat the cream in a small saucepan until almost boiling, then remove from the heat. Sprinkle the powdered gelatine over, stirring until completely dissolved.

4 Then pour on to the chocolate mixture, whisking vigorously to mix until smooth.

5 Whisk the yogurt and vanilla essence into the mixture. In a clean, grease-free bowl, whisk the egg whites until stiff, then fold them into the mixture. Tip the mixture into the prepared loaf tin, level the surface and chill until set.

6 Make the sauce. Melt the chocolate with the rum and cream in a heatproof bowl over barely simmering water, stirring occasionally. Leave to cool completely.

7 When the mousse is set, remove it from the tin with the aid of the paper or clear film. Serve in thick slices with the cooled chocolate sauce poured around.

THESE **RICH LITTLE POTS**, PREPARED IN ADVANCE, ARE THE **PERFECT ENDING** TO A DINNER PARTY. FOR THE **VERY BEST FLAVOUR**, REMOVE THEM FROM THE FRIDGE ABOUT 30 MINUTES **BEFORE SERVING**, TO ALLOW THEM TO "**RIPEN**".

ingredients

250g/9oz **plain chocolate**
60ml/4 tbsp **Madeira**
25g/1oz/2 tbsp **butter**, diced
2 **eggs**, separated
225g/8oz/1 cup unsweetened
    chestnut purée
crème fraîche or whipped
    double cream, to decorate

chocolate & chestnut pots

method

SERVES 6

1 Make a few chocolate curls for decoration, then break the rest of the chocolate into squares and melt it with the Madeira in a saucepan over a gentle heat. Remove from the heat and add the butter, a few pieces at a time, stirring until melted and smooth.

2 Beat the egg yolks quickly into the mixture, then beat in the chestnut purée, mixing until smooth.

3 Whisk the egg whites in a clean, grease-free bowl until stiff. Stir about 15ml/1tbsp of the whites into the chestnut mixture to lighten it, then fold in the rest evenly.

4 Spoon the mixture into six small ramekin dishes and chill until set. Serve the pots topped with a generous spoonful of crème fraîche or whipped double cream. Decorate with the plain chocolate curls.

cook's tip
If Madeira is not available, use brandy or rum instead. These chocolate pots can be frozen successfully for up to 2 months.

chocolate cones with apricot sauce

THE **SEDUCTIVE LIAISON** OF **SMOOTH DARK** CHOCOLATE AND **BRANDY-FLAVOURED** CREAM MAKES A **DRAMATIC** AND **DELICIOUS** DESSERT.

method

SERVES 6

1 Cut 12 x 10cm/4in double thickness rounds from non-stick baking paper and shape each into a cone. Secure with masking tape.

2 Melt the chocolate in a heatproof bowl set over a pan of simmering water. Leave the melted chocolate to cool slightly.

3 Spoon a little of the cooled chocolate into each cone, swirling and brushing it to coat the paper in an even layer.

4 Stand each cone point downwards in a cup or glass, to hold it straight. Leave in a cool place until the cones are completely set.

5 Make the sauce. Combine the apricot jam and lemon juice in a small saucepan. Melt over a gentle heat, then cool.

6 Beat the ricotta, cream, brandy and icing sugar in a bowl. Stir in the lemon rind.

7 Spoon or pipe the ricotta mixture into the cones, then carefully peel off the baking paper.

8 Serve the cones in pairs on individual plates, scattered with lemon rind and surrounded with the cooled apricot sauce.

ingredients

250g/9oz **plain dark chocolate**, broken into squares
350g/12oz/1½ cups **ricotta cheese**
45ml/3 tbsp **double cream**
30ml/2 tbsp **brandy**
30ml/2 tbsp **icing sugar**
finely grated rind of 1 **lemon**
strips of **lemon rind**, to decorate

For the sauce
175g/6oz/⅔ cup **apricot jam**
45ml/3 tbsp **lemon juice**

cook's tip
When making the paper cones, make sure there is no gap at the pointed end or the chocolate will run out when you coat them. It is best to let the chocolate cool slightly before use, so that it sets quickly.

devilish chocolate roulade

A **DECADENT DESSERT** FOR A **DINNER À DEUX** OR A **PARTY**. THE ROULADE CAN BE MADE A **DAY OR TWO** AHEAD, THEN **FILLED** AND **ROLLED** ON THE DAY OF SERVING.

ingredients

175g/6oz **plain dark chocolate**, broken into squares
4 **eggs**, separated
115g/4oz/1/2 cup **caster sugar**
cocoa powder, for dusting

For the filling
225g/8oz **plain chocolate**, broken into squares
45ml/3 tbsp **brandy**
2 **eggs**, separated
250g/9oz/generous 1cup **mascarpone cheese**
chocolate-dipped strawberries, to decorate

---

cook's tip
Don't worry if the roulade cracks – it's meant to!

---

method

SERVES 6–8

1 Preheat the oven to 180°C/350°F/Gas 4. Grease a 33 x 23cm/ 13 x 9in Swiss roll tin and line with non-stick baking paper. Melt the chocolate in a heatproof bowl.

2 Whisk the egg yolks and sugar in a bowl until pale and thick, then stir in the melted chocolate evenly.

3 In a clean, grease-free bowl, whisk the egg whites to soft peaks, then fold lightly and evenly into the egg and chocolate mixture.

4 Scrape into the tin and spread evenly to the corners. Bake for 15–20 minutes, until the sponge is well risen and firm to the touch. Dust a sheet of non-stick baking paper with cocoa. Turn the sponge out on the paper, cover with a clean dish towel and leave to cool.

5 Make the filling. Melt the chocolate with the brandy in a heatproof bowl over hot water. Remove from the heat. Beat the egg yolks together, then beat into the chocolate mixture. In a separate bowl, whisk the whites to soft peaks, then fold them lightly and evenly into the filling.

6 Uncover the roulade, remove the lining paper and spread with the mascarpone. Spread the chocolate mixture over the top, then roll up carefully from a long side to enclose the filling. Transfer to a serving plate, top with fresh chocolate-dipped strawberries and dust with cocoa powder.

chocolate pavlova with passion fruit cream

PASSION FRUIT IS CERTAINLY **APTLY NAMED**. SERVE THIS **SUPERB** DESSERT AND **ANYTHING** COULD HAPPEN.

ingredients

4 **egg whites**
200g/7oz/scant 1 cup
  caster sugar
20ml/4 tsp **cornflour**
45ml/3 tbsp **cocoa powder**
5ml/1 tsp **vinegar**
chocolate leaves, to decorate

For the filling
150g/5oz **plain chocolate**
  broken into squares
250ml/8fl oz/1 cup
  double cream
150g/5oz/2/3 cup **Greek-style yogurt**
2.5ml/1/2 tsp **vanilla essence**
4 **passion fruit**

---

cook's tip
The meringue can be baked a day in advance and stored in an airtight container. Do not add the filling until an hour before serving.

---

method

SERVES 6

1 Preheat the oven to 140°C/275°F/Gas 1. Cut a piece of non-stick baking paper to fit a baking sheet. Draw a 23cm/9in circle on the paper and place it upside down on the baking sheet.

2 Whisk the egg whites in a clean, grease-free bowl until stiff. Gradually whisk in the sugar and continue to whisk until the mixture is stiff again. Whisk in the cornflour, cocoa and vinegar.

3 Spread the mixture over the marked circle, making a slight dip in the centre. Bake in the oven for 1 1/2–2 hours.

4 Make the filling. Melt the chocolate in a heatproof bowl over hot water, then remove from the heat and allow the chocolate to cool slightly. In a separate bowl, whip the cream with the yogurt and vanilla essence until thick. Fold 60ml/4 tbsp of the cream mixture into the chocolate, then set both mixtures aside.

5 Halve all the passion fruit and scoop out the pulp. Stir half into the plain cream mixture. Carefully remove the meringue shell from the baking sheet and place it on a large serving plate. Fill with the passion fruit cream, then spoon over the chocolate mixture and the remaining passion fruit.

6 Decorate the pavlova with chocolate leaves before serving.

italian chocolate ricotta pie

THIS **GLORIOUS** PIE **TRAVELS WELL** AND IS **PERFECT** FOR ELEGANT **SUMMER PICNICS**.

method

SERVES 6

1 Preheat the oven to 200°C/400°F/Gas 6. Sift the flour and cocoa into a bowl, then stir in the sugar. Rub in the butter until the mixture resembles breadcrumbs, then work in the sherry, using your fingertips, until the mixture binds to a firm dough.

2 Roll out three-quarters of the pastry on a lightly floured surface and line a 24cm/9^1/2in loose-based flan tin.

3 Make the filling. Beat the egg yolks and sugar in a bowl, then beat in the ricotta to mix thoroughly. Stir in the lemon rind, chocolate chips, mixed peel and angelica.

4 Scrape the ricotta mixture into the pastry case and level the surface. Roll out the remaining pastry and cut into strips, then arrange these in a lattice over the pie.

5 Bake for 15 minutes, then lower the oven temperature to 180°C/350°F/Gas 4 and cook for a further 30–35 minutes, until golden brown and firm. Cool in the tin.

---

cook's tip
This pie is best served at room temperature, so if you make it in advance, chill it when cool, then bring to room temperature for about 30 minutes before serving.

---

ingredients

225g/8oz/2 cups **plain flour**
30ml/2 tbsp **cocoa powder**
60ml/4 tbsp **caster sugar**
115g/4oz/^{1}/2 cup **unsalted butter**
60ml/4 tbsp **dry sherry**

For the filling
2 **egg yolks**
115g/4oz/^{1}/2 cup **caster sugar**
500g/1^1/4lb/2^1/2 cups **ricotta cheese**
finely grated rind of 1 **lemon**
90ml/6 tbsp **plain dark chocolate chips**
75ml/5 tbsp chopped **mixed peel**
45ml/3 tbsp chopped **angelica**

ingredients

250g/9oz/2¼ cups **plain flour**
150g/5oz/⅔ cup **unsalted butter**
2 **egg yolks**
15–30ml/1–2 tbsp **iced water**

For the filling
3 **eggs**, separated
20ml/4 tsp **cornflour**
75g/3oz/⅓ cup golden **caster sugar**
400ml/14fl oz/1¾ cups **milk**
150g/5oz **plain chocolate**, broken into squares
5ml/1 tsp **vanilla essence**
1 sachet powdered **gelatine**
45ml/3 tbsp **water**
30ml/2 tbsp **dark rum**

For the topping
175ml/6fl oz/¾ cup **double** or **whipping cream**
chocolate curls

mississippi mud pie

MUD, **MUD**, GLORIOUS **MUD** — ISN'T THAT WHAT THE **SONG** SAYS? WELL, THEY DON'T COME **MUCH MORE GLORIOUS** THAN THIS.

method

SERVES 6–8

1 Sift the flour into a bowl and rub in the butter until the mixture resembles coarse breadcrumbs. Stir in the egg yolks with just enough iced water to bind the mixture to a soft dough. Roll out on a lightly floured surface and line a deep 23cm/9in flan tin. Chill for about 30 minutes.

2 Preheat the oven to 190°C/375°F/Gas 5. Prick the pastry case all over with a fork, cover with greaseproof paper weighed down with baking beans and bake blind for 10 minutes. Remove the baking beans and paper, return to the oven and bake for a further 10 minutes, until the pastry is crisp and golden. Cool in the tin.

3 Make the filling. Mix the egg yolks, cornflour and 30ml/2 tbsp of the sugar in a bowl. Heat the milk in a saucepan until almost boiling, then beat into the egg mixture. Return to the clean pan and stir over a low heat until the custard has thickened and is smooth. Pour half the custard into a bowl.

4 Melt the chocolate in a heatproof bowl over hot water, then stir into the custard in the bowl, with the vanilla essence. Spread in the pastry case, cover closely to prevent the formation of a skin. Leave to cool, then chill until set.

5 Sprinkle the gelatine over the water in a small bowl, leave until spongy, then place over simmering water until all the gelatine has dissolved. Stir into the remaining custard, with the rum. Whisk the egg whites in a clean, grease-free bowl until stiff peaks form, whisk in the remaining sugar, then fold quickly into the custard before it sets.

6 Spoon the mixture over the chocolate custard to cover completely. Chill until set, then remove the pie from the tin and place on a serving plate. Spread whipped cream over the top and sprinkle with chocolate curls.

chocolate orange marquise

THERE ARE **PEOPLE** WHO **QUITE LIKE** CHOCOLATE, **OTHERS** WHO **ENJOY** IT **NOW** AND **AGAIN**, AND **SOME** WHO ARE **UTTERLY PASSIONATE** ABOUT THE STUFF. IF YOU FALL INTO THE **FINAL CATEGORY**, YOU'LL **SIMPLY ADORE** THIS **DREAM** DESSERT.

ingredients

200g/7oz/scant 1 cup **caster sugar**
60ml/4 tbsp freshly squeezed **orange juice**
350g/12oz **plain dark chocolate**, broken into squares
225g/8oz/1 cup **unsalted butter**, cubed
5 **eggs**
finely grated rind of 1 **orange**
45ml/3 tbsp **plain flour**
icing sugar and finely pared strips of **orange rind**, to decorate

cook's tip

The safest way to add the water to the roasting tin is to place the tin on a shelf in the oven, pull the shelf out slightly, then pour in freshly boiled water from a kettle. If you pour the water in before transferring the tin to the oven, there is always a risk of spills and scalds.

method

SERVES 6–8

1 Preheat the oven to 180°C/350°F/Gas 4. Grease a 23cm/9in round cake tin with a depth of 6cm/2½in. Line the base with non-stick baking paper.

2 Place 115g/4oz/½ cup of the sugar in a saucepan. Add the orange juice and stir over a gentle heat until the sugar has dissolved.

3 Remove from the heat and stir in the chocolate until melted, then add the butter, cube by cube, until thoroughly melted and evenly mixed.

4 Whisk the eggs with the remaining sugar in a large bowl until pale and very thick. Add the orange rind. Then, using a metal spoon, fold the chocolate mixture lightly and evenly into the egg mixture. Sift the flour over the top and fold in evenly.

5 Scrape the mixture into the prepared tin. Place in a roasting tin, transfer to the oven, then pour hot water into the roasting tin to reach about halfway up the sides of the cake tin.

6 Bake for about 1 hour, or until the cake is firm to the touch. Remove the cake tin from the roasting tin and cool for 15–20 minutes. To turn out, invert the cake on a baking sheet, place a serving plate upside down on top, then turn plate and baking sheet over together so that the cake is transferred to the plate.

7 Dust with icing sugar, decorate with strips of pared orange rind and serve slightly warm or cold.

raspberry & white chocolate cheesecake

RASPBERRIES AND **WHITE CHOCOLATE** MAKE AN **IRRESISTIBLE** COMBINATION, ESPECIALLY WHEN **TEAMED** WITH **RICH** AND **CREAMY** **MASCARPONE** ON A CRUNCHY **GINGER** AND **PECAN NUT** BASE.

ingredients

method

SERVES 8

50g/2oz/4 tbsp **unsalted butter**
225g/8oz **ginger nut biscuits**, crushed
50g/2oz/1/2 cup chopped **pecan nuts** or **walnuts**

For the filling
275g/10oz/11/4 cups **mascarpone cheese**
175g/6oz/3/4 cup **fromage frais**
2 **eggs**, beaten
45ml/3 tbsp **caster sugar**
250g/9oz **white chocolate**, broken into squares
225g/8oz/11/2 cups fresh or frozen **raspberries**

For the topping
115g/4oz/1/2 cup **mascarpone cheese**
75g/3oz/1/3 cup **fromage frais**
white chocolate curls and **raspberries**, to decorate

1 Preheat the oven to 150°C/300°F/Gas 2. Melt the butter in a saucepan, then stir in the crushed biscuits and nuts. Press into the base of a 23cm/9in springform cake tin.

2 Make the filling. Beat the mascarpone and fromage frais in a bowl, then beat in the eggs and caster sugar until evenly mixed.

3 Melt the white chocolate gently in a heatproof bowl over hot water, then stir into the cheese mixture with the fresh or frozen raspberries.

4 Tip into the prepared tin and spread evenly, then bake for about 1 hour or until just set. Switch off the oven, but do not remove the cheesecake. Leave it until cold and completely set.

5 Remove the sides of the tin and carefully lift the cheesecake on to a serving plate. Make the topping by mixing the mascarpone and fromage frais in a bowl and spreading the mixture over the cheesecake. Decorate with white chocolate curls and raspberries.

cook's tip
The biscuits for the base should be crushed quite finely. This can easily be done in a food processor. Alternatively, place the biscuits in a stout plastic bag and crush them with a rolling pin.

sweets & drinks

malt whisky truffles

method

THESE **TEMPTING** TRUFFLES MAKE **PERFECT PRESENTS** – IF YOU CAN **PART** WITH THEM.

ingredients

200g/7oz **plain dark chocolate**, broken into squares

115g/4oz/1 cup **icing sugar**

150ml/¼ pint/⅔ cup **double cream**

45ml/3 tbsp **malt whisky**

cocoa powder, for coating

1 Melt the squares of chocolate in a heatproof bowl set over a pan of simmering water, then set aside to cool slightly.

2 Whip the cream with the whisky in a bowl until it is thick enough to hold its shape.

3 Stir the chocolate and icing sugar into the whisky cream. Leave until the mixture is firm enough to handle.

4 Dust your hands with cocoa and shape the mixture into bite-size balls. Roll in cocoa powder and pack into pretty cases or boxes. The truffles can be stored in the fridge for up to 3–4 days.

chocolate fondant hearts

method

MAKES ABOUT 50

GET SET TO **IMPRESS** THE OBJECT OF YOUR **HEART'S DESIRE** WITH THESE **LUSCIOUS** CHOCOLATE **LOVE TOKENS**.

ingredients

60ml/4 tbsp **liquid glucose**

50g/2oz **plain dark chocolate**, broken into squares

50g/2oz **white chocolate**, broken into squares

1 **egg white**, lightly beaten

450g/1lb/3½ cups **icing sugar**, sifted

melted **plain dark** and **white chocolate**, to decorate

1 Divide the glucose between two heatproof bowls. Place each bowl over hot water and heat the glucose gently, then add the dark chocolate to one bowl and the white chocolate to the other. Leave until the chocolate has completely melted.

2 Remove both bowls from the heat and cool slightly. Divide half the egg white between the bowls, then divide the icing sugar between them, mixing to combine well.

3 Knead each mixture separately with your hands until it is smooth and pliable. On a surface lightly dusted with icing sugar, roll out both mixtures separately to a thickness of about 3mm/⅛in.

4 Brush the surface of the dark chocolate fondant with egg white and place the white chocolate fondant on top. Roll the surface lightly with a rolling pin to press the pieces together.

5 Using a small heart-shaped cutter, stamp out about 50 hearts from the fondant. Drizzle melted chocolate over each heart to decorate and leave until firm.

chocolate almond torrone

SERVE THIS **WICKEDLY RICH** SPANISH **SPECIALITY** IN THIN SLICES.

ingredients

method

SERVES 6

115g/4oz **plain dark chocolate**, broken into squares

50g/2oz/4 tbsp **unsalted butter**

1 **egg white**

115g/4oz/1/2 cup **caster sugar**

50g/2oz/1/2 cup **ground almonds**

75g/3oz/1/2 cup chopped **toasted almonds**

75ml/5 tbsp chopped **candied peel**

For the coating

175g/6oz **white chocolate**, broken into squares

25g/1oz/2 tbsp **unsalted butter**

115g/4oz/1 cup **flaked almonds**, toasted

1 Melt the chocolate with the butter in a heatproof bowl set over a pan of barely simmering water.

2 In a clean, grease-free bowl, whisk the egg white with the sugar until stiff. Gradually beat in the melted chocolate, then stir in the ground almonds, chopped toasted almonds and peel.

3 Tip the mixture on to a large sheet of non-stick baking paper and shape into a thick roll.

4 As the mixture cools, use the paper to press the roll into a triangular shape. Twist the paper over the triangular roll and chill until set.

5 Make the coating. Melt the white chocolate with the butter in a heatproof bowl over hot water. Unwrap the chocolate roll and spread the white chocolate quickly over the surface. Press the almonds in a thin, even coating over the chocolate, working quickly before the chocolate sets.

6 Chill in the fridge again until firm, then cut the torrone into fairly thin slices to serve.

---

cook's tip
The mixture can be shaped into a simple round roll instead of the triangular shape if you prefer.

ingredients

250g/9oz/generous 1 cup
granulated sugar
375g/13oz can **sweetened
condensed milk**
50g/2oz/4 tbsp **unsalted butter**
5ml/1 tsp **vanilla essence**
115g/4oz **plain dark
chocolate**, grated
75g/3oz/¾ cup **pistachios**,
almonds or **hazelnuts**

rich chocolate pistachio fudge

MAKE A **BIG BATCH** OF THIS **MELTINGLY**
RICH CHOCOLATE FUDGE **PACKED** WITH
PISTACHIOS – IT WON'T LAST LONG!

method

MAKES 20–24

1 Grease a 19cm/7½in square cake tin and line with non-stick baking
paper. Mix the sugar, condensed milk and butter in a heavy-based
pan. Heat gently, stirring the mixture occasionally, until the sugar has
dissolved completely.

2 Bring the mixture to the boil, stirring occasionally, and boil until it
registers 116°C/240°F on a sugar thermometer (see cook's tip).

3 Remove the pan from the heat and beat in the vanilla essence,
chocolate and nuts. Beat vigorously until the mixture is smooth and
creamy.

4 Pour the mixture into the prepared cake tin and spread evenly. Leave
until just set, then mark into squares. Leave to set completely before
cutting into squares and removing from the tin. Store in an airtight
container in a cool place.

cook's tip
If you haven't got a sugar thermometer, test the mixture by dropping a small
spoonful into a cup of iced water. If you can roll the mixture to a soft ball with
your fingertips, the fudge is ready.

chocolate-coated nut brittle

TAKE **EQUAL AMOUNTS** OF **PECAN NUTS** AND **ALMONDS**, SET THEM IN **CRISP CARAMEL**, THEN ADD A **DARK** CHOCOLATE COATING FOR A **SWEET** THAT'S **TRULY SENSATIONAL**.

method

MAKES 20–24

1 Lightly grease a baking sheet with butter or oil. Mix the nuts, sugar and water in a heavy-based saucepan. Place the pan over a gentle heat, stirring, without boiling, until the sugar has dissolved.

2 Bring to the boil, then lower the heat to moderate and cook until the mixture turns a rich golden brown and registers 148°C/300°F on a sugar thermometer. To test without a thermometer, drop a few drops of the mixture into a cup of iced water. The mixture should become brittle enough to snap with your fingers.

3 Quickly remove the pan from the heat and tip the mixture on to the prepared baking sheet, spreading it evenly. Leave until completely cold and hard.

4 Break the nut brittle into bite-size pieces. Melt the chocolate in a heatproof bowl over hot water and dip the pieces to half-coat them. Leave on a sheet of non-stick baking paper to set.

cook's tip
Brittle looks best in rough chunks, so don't worry if the pieces break unevenly, or if there are gaps in the chocolate.

ingredients

115g/4oz/1 cup mixed **pecan nuts** and whole **almonds**
115g/4oz/¹⁄₂ cup **caster sugar**
60ml/4 tbsp **water**
200g/7oz **plain dark chocolate**, broken into squares

ingredients

115g/4oz **plain dark chocolate**, broken into squares

75g/3oz **white or milk chocolate**, broken into squares

25g/1oz/2 tbsp **unsalted butter**, melted

15ml/1 tbsp **kirsch** or **brandy**

60ml/4 tbsp **double cream**

18–20 **maraschino cherries** or **liqueur-soaked cherries**

chocolate & cherry colettes

FOR A **SWEET SURPRISE**, PACK THESE **PRETTY** LITTLE SWEETS IN A **DECORATIVE BOX** FOR A **FRIEND** OR **LOVER**.

method

MAKES 20

1 Melt the dark chocolate in a bowl over hot water, then remove from the heat. Spoon into 18–20 foil sweet cases, spread evenly up the sides with a small brush, then leave in a cool place to set.

2 Melt the white or milk chocolate with the butter in a heatproof bowl over hot water. Remove from the heat and stir in the kirsch or brandy, then the cream. Cool until the mixture is thick enough to hold its shape.

3 Place one maraschino or liqueur-soaked cherry in each chocolate case. Spoon the white or milk chocolate cream mixture into a piping bag fitted with a small star nozzle and pipe over the cherries, mounding the cream mixture in a generous swirl.

4 Top each colette with a chocolate curl. Leave until set, then chill in the fridge until needed.

cook's tip
If foil sweet cases are difficult to obtain, you can use double thickness paper sweet cases instead.

cognac & ginger creams

ONLY YOU KNOW THE **SECRET** OF THESE **HANDSOME** HANDMADE CHOCOLATES: THAT THE **MYSTERIOUS DARK** EXTERIOR CONCEALS A **GLORIOUS GINGER** AND **COGNAC CREAM** FILLING.

method

MAKES 18–20

1 Polish the insides of about 18–20 chocolate moulds with cotton wool. Melt about two-thirds of the chocolate in a heatproof bowl over hot water, then spoon a little into each mould. Reserve a little of the melted chocolate, for sealing the creams.

2 Using a small brush, sweep the chocolate up the sides of the moulds to coat them evenly, then invert them on to a sheet of greaseproof paper and leave to set.

3 Melt the remaining chocolate, then stir in the cream, cognac, ginger syrup and stem ginger, mixing well. Spoon into the chocolate-lined moulds. Warm the reserved chocolate if necessary, then spoon a little into each mould to seal. Leave in a cool place, but not the fridge, until set.

4 To remove the chocolates from the moulds, gently press them out on to a cool surface. Decorate with small pieces of crystallized ginger.

cook's tip
Simple chocolate moulds can be bought in most good kitchen shops and give a highly professional finish. Polishing the moulds thoroughly with fine cotton wool results in really glossy chocolates that are relatively easy to turn out. If they do stick, put them in the fridge for a short time, then try again. Don't chill them for too long, or you may dull the surface of the chocolate.

ingredients

300g/11oz **plain dark chocolate**, broken into squares
45ml/3 tbsp **double cream**
30ml/2 tbsp **cognac**
15ml/1 tbsp **stem ginger syrup**
4 pieces **stem ginger**, finely chopped
crystallized ginger, to decorate

mexican hot chocolate

SNUGGLE DOWN IN BED WITH A **BIG MUG** OF **DELICIOUSLY SPICY** HOT CHOCOLATE. IN **MEXICO**, THIS DRINK IS **TRADITIONALLY** WHISKED WITH A CARVED WOODEN BEATER CALLED A **MOLINILLO**, BUT A **MODERN BLENDER** WORKS JUST AS WELL.

ingredients

1 litre/1¾ pints/4 cups semi-
  skimmed **milk**
1 **cinnamon stick**
2 **whole cloves**

115g/4oz **plain dark
  chocolate**, broken into
  squares
2–3 drops of **almond essence**

method

SERVES 4

1 Heat the milk gently with the spices in a saucepan until almost boiling, then stir in the plain chocolate over a moderate heat until melted.

2 Strain into a blender, add the almond essence and process on high speed for about 30 seconds, until frothy. Alternatively, whisk the mixture with a hand-held electric mixer or wire whisk.

3 Pour into heatproof glasses and serve immediately.

---

cook's tip
If you don't have whole cinnamon and cloves, add a pinch of each of the ground spices to the mixture.

---

peppermint chocolate sticks

TURN THE **LIGHTS DOWN** LOW, **CURL UP** ON THE COUCH AND **PAMPER YOURSELF** WITH THESE **DELICIOUS BITE-SIZE** CHOCOLATE STICKS.

ingredients

115g/4oz/½ cup
  granulated sugar
150ml/¼ pint/⅔ cup **water**
2.5ml/½ tsp **peppermint
  essence**

200g/7oz **plain dark
  chocolate**, broken into
  squares
60ml/4 tbsp **toasted
  desiccated coconut**

---

cook's tip
The set chocolate mixture could be cut into squares instead, to eat just as they are or for decorating cakes and desserts.

---

method

MAKES ABOUT 80

1 Lightly oil a large baking sheet. Place the sugar and water in a small, heavy-based saucepan and heat gently, stirring occasionally, until the sugar has dissolved completely.

2 Bring to the boil and boil rapidly without stirring until the syrup registers 137°C/280°F on a sugar thermometer. Remove the pan from the heat and add the peppermint essence, then pour on to the greased baking sheet and leave until set and completely cold.

3 Break up the peppermint mixture into a small bowl and use the end of a rolling pin to crush it into small pieces.

4 Melt the chocolate in a heatproof bowl over hot water. Remove from the heat and stir in the mint pieces and desiccated coconut.

5 Lay a 30 x 25cm/12 x 10in sheet of non-stick baking paper on a flat surface. Spread the chocolate mixture over the paper, leaving a narrow border all around, to make a rectangle measuring about 25 x 20cm/ 10 x 8in. Leave to set. When firm, use a sharp knife to cut into thin sticks, each about 6cm/2½in long

irish chocolate velvet

method

SERVES 4

WARM THE COCKLES OF YOUR **HEART** WITH THIS **SMOOTH**, **SOPHISTICATED** COCKTAIL.

ingredients

120ml/4fl oz/1/2 cup **double cream**
400ml/14fl oz/13/4 cups **milk**
115g/4oz **milk chocolate**, broken into squares

30ml/2 tbsp **cocoa powder**
60ml/4 tbsp **Irish whiskey**
whipped cream, for topping
chocolate curls, to decorate

1 Whip the cream in a bowl until it is thick enough to hold its shape.

2 Place the milk and chocolate in a heavy-based saucepan and heat gently, stirring, until the chocolate has melted.

3 Whisk in the cocoa, then bring to the boil, remove from the heat and add the cream and Irish whiskey.

4 Pour quickly into four heatproof mugs or glasses and top each serving with a generous spoonful of whipped cream. Decorate with chocolate curls and serve.

cook's tip
If Irish whiskey is not available, use Scotch whisky, brandy or a liqueur based on either.

iced mint & chocolate cooler

method

SERVES 4

MANY **CHOCOLATE DRINKS** ARE **WARM** AND **COMFORTING**, BUT THIS ONE IS DELICIOUSLY **REFRESHING**. IT IS **IDEAL** FOR A **HOT SUMMER'S DAY**.

ingredients

60ml/4 tbsp **drinking chocolate**
400ml/14fl oz/13/4 cups chilled **milk**
150ml/1/4 pint/2/3 cup **natural yogurt**

2.5ml/1/2 tsp **peppermint essence**
4 scoops **chocolate ice cream**
mint leaves and **chocolate shapes**, to decorate

1 Place the drinking chocolate in a small saucepan and stir in about 120ml/4fl oz/1/2 cup of the milk. Heat gently, stirring, until almost boiling, then remove from the heat.

2 Pour into a cold bowl or large jug and whisk in the remaining milk, yogurt and peppermint essence.

3 Pour the mixture into four chilled, tall glasses and top each with a scoop of ice cream. Decorate with mint leaves and chocolate shapes. Serve immediately.

cook's tip
Use could cocoa powder instead of drinking chocolate if you prefer, but you would need to add sugar to taste.

index